The Journey to a New Start

Wilfred Stewart

Copyright © 2024 by Wilfred Stewart.

ISBN: 979-8-89090-238-2 (sc)
ISBN: 979-8-89090-239-9 (eb)

All rights reserved. No part of this book may be reproduced or transmitted in any form or by any means, electronic or mechanical, including photocopying, recording, or by any information storage and retrieval system, without permission in writing from the copyright owner.

The views expressed in this work are solely those of the author and do not necessarily reflect the views of the publisher, and the publisher hereby disclaims any responsibility for them.

EXPRESSO
Executive Center 777, Dunsmuir Street Vancouver, BC V71K4
1-888-721-0662 ext 101
info@expressopublishing.com

TABLE OF CONTENTS

Growing up as a kid 1

Going to high school 12

Going to ebony park 19

Going to agriculture college case 28

Working a full-time job... 33

Working on the cruise ship 53

A message... 70

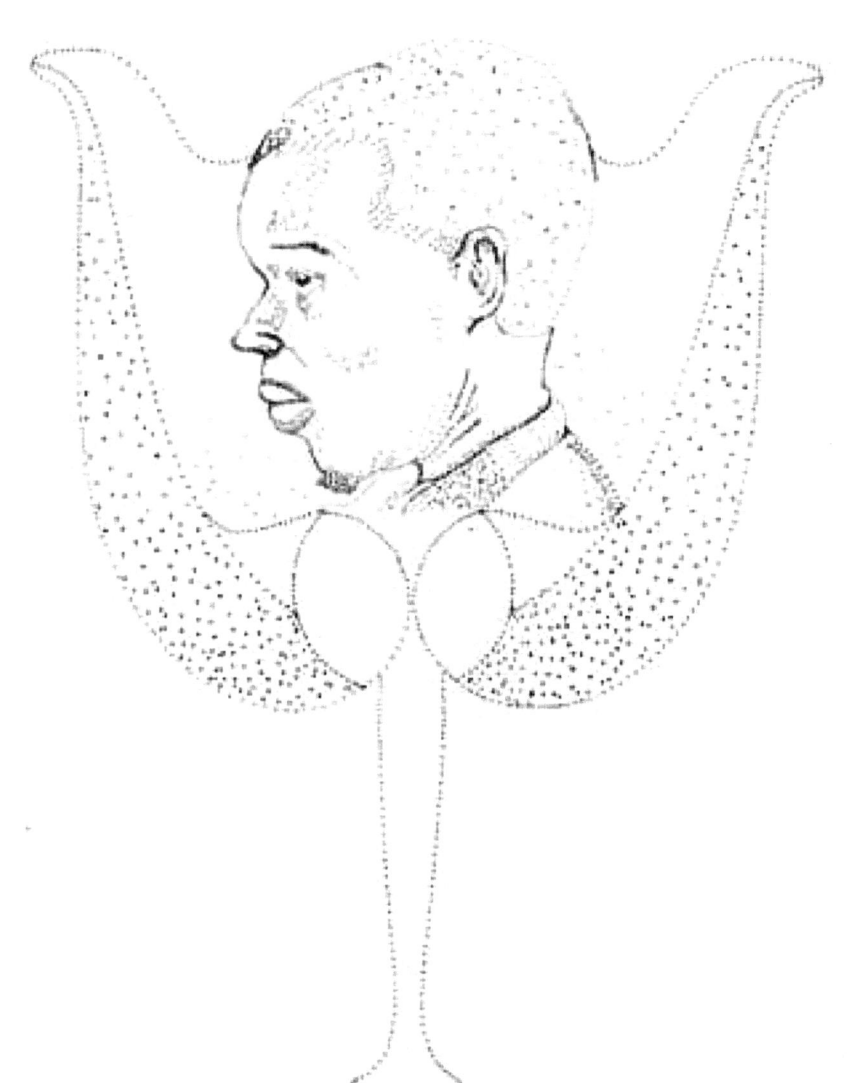

GROWING UP AS A KID

I was born and raised in Jamaica, in the city of Clarendon, in a small community called John's Hall. John's Hall is known because of its farming, such as sugarcane, citrus, coffee, and mangoes. However, Jamaica on the other hand is known because of its tourism, bauxite, and tropical climate.

During my childhood, it was very hard for me growing up as a kid. My parents weren't living together. My father had separated from my mother. He was living in the same community but in a different address. At that time, I was the sixth child of my mother; then she went on to have two more kids.

It was hard for her to take care of all of us because her second kid, which is her oldest son, was paralyzed. He could not talk or move around, so she had to do everything for him. Also, there wasn't a lot of job opportunities in the community for her to get employed so she could support us. The easiest job she could get is to go and work in the field when it is harvesttime.

Even though she had those other children, she wasn't getting any help from their fathers. My father was in a better job than my mother. He was working at the police station in Frank field, the closest town to John's Hall, which is about five miles away. My father's job is basically to make sure the people in the community of John's Hall abide by the rules and regulation of the police. So whatever happens in the community, the people have to report to him first, and then he would go and investigate the matter and then report the matter to the police. When it comes to weekends, my mother would make sure that I go and visit my father. My next older brother, Dixie, would go with me to my father's house. My father would make sure to give me some money, and he also packed a bag for me with yam, banana, sugarcane, breadfruit, and oranges. As it reaches the time for us to leave, my brother Dixie would put the bag on his head; we'd both leave for home. We walked about one mile to reach home.

Farming is not a big issue in John's Hall, but it becomes one when it reaches the time for the produce to be sold. The biggest problem the farmers have to deal with is transportation. At that time, we only had one bus that runs at approximately 5:00 am, and it comes back at about 7:00 pm the same day. Everyone who is going to far distances would have to make sure that they get up very early to get ready so that they can catch the bus.

It was hard for all those children going to high school, like Clarendon College, Glenmuir, and Vere Technical. That one bus has to carry passengers from maybe four to five other communities to the nearest town so that we could have easy access to other transportation to take us to our next destination. Because it was the only bus that time of the morning, the farmers had to take the bus along with the school children.

Traveling on the bus was not easy; the reason was it had five people working on it—two on the ground picked up the produce, giving it to two other persons on top of the bus. The other person worked inside the bus, collecting the fare; the bus was built with a carrier on top of it to carry load.

Sometimes when there were a lot of produce going out in the morning, the load on top of the bus might be about two feet tall.

While the top of the bus was overloaded, the inside had its own issues of overcrowding. The bus capacity was about fifty passengers seated. However, the bus would have double the number of seated passenger standing. It was so packed, and passengers were standing on the step with parts of their limbs hanging outside. We knew that it was very dangerous; the road was so narrow and small. If the bus made a wrong turn, we all would die. But we have no other way to get out when it comes to transportation. When the children reached the school, they couldn't stand on their feet; they had bad blood circulation from standing in awkward positions. Also their uniforms got crushed and their shoes dirty.

During that time, there were no washing machines, and if there was any, no one in my community could afford one. So people would always call my mother to wash some clothes. My mother, Jane Doyley, would wash some clothes with her hands to get money for us to survive. She washed so many clothes her fingers got sores and developed a thing, whitlow, because her finger was soaked too much in water. It is not easy to wash those thick jeans, especially the ones the farmers wore to the farm; because they spent a lot of time playing outside, even the clothes that the kids wore are hard to wash.

Then came this gentle man by the name of Brenton Reid, someone who many people in the community respect. For one reason, he is a minister of one of the churches in the community. Next, he has a lot of property and livestock, so he always has some work for people who want to work in the agricultural field. When the washing wasn't working out for my mom, she decided to go and ask Mr. Reid for some work on his farm. She was lucky and got the job at the time of harvest.

Oftentimes when it comes to harvesttime, even though my father still worked with the Frank field police, he would still work for Mr. Reid. When I was five years old, I remember the first day my brother Dixie took me to school. My mom cut my pencil and notebook in half. There are two reasons why she had to cut them—one, she always saves something for the next day; next, she had to save the other half for one of the other children. Another thing happened to me on the first day of school. It was playtime, and I went outside to play. While I was taking a time-out, the ants kept on attracting my feet because I wasn't wearing any shoes, and my mom used some cooking oil and rubbed my feet with it, only because she could not afford skin lotion. Even though she was working, the money was small, just enough to buy food.

Also, I could wear my shoes only to church or if I was going to the doctor. When I do get a pair of shoes, my mom would make sure that it is larger than the size I wear, that two years down the road, I still can fit those shoes. Furthermore, I realized more and more what is going on in my life. I started to see my mom sitting down with her hand on her head, wondering. About what, I don't know—maybe she was thinking what our next meal was going to be or who is going to call her to work the next day. I really wanted to help her, but there is little I can do. Sometimes when we come up short, we only drink water and say our prayer before we go to sleep and ask God to save our lives so we could see another day. For that is the greatest thing—life.

Although there were many nights we went to bed without eating, there was this neighbor who had a grandson. We were of the same age, went to the same school, and were in the same class. We played after school; sometimes he came to my house or I would go to his house. However, I was the one going to his house most of the time; oftentimes his grandmother gave me something to eat. It reached a point where if I am not over his house, I can still stay at my house and know whether she was cooking or not. At that time, she did not have a gas stove; she cooked on the wood fire. So when she first started cooking, the smoke was very thick and dark; when the smoke got lighter and I heard her reaching for the dishes, I knew that she was finished cooking.

After all those observations, I took my time and went to my friend's house; as soon as I reached there, she would fix a plate for me. I was doing it for a long time; then one evening after school, it was just the right time she finished cooking dinner. She gave me a plate, and I started eating; about five minutes later, I was finished eating and gave her the empty plate. She stared at me; I knew that something was wrong. I was in a state of paralysis for a few minutes, but at the same time, I was optimistic. She called me over, "Come here, Basil." I went to her; she asked me, "What is that in your pocket?" I was speechless. She stuck her hand in my pocket and pulled out the food and meat from my pocket; all the grease from the food was just streaming down my feet. She looked at me and shook her head.

After that happened, she asked me why I was doing this. I told her that my mother doesn't have anything for us to eat, and I want to take it to her so that she can share it with the rest of the family. She eventually started making my plate bigger and had me take it to my mother every evening even if I was not there. While growing up, I faced a lot of hard time. For example, I could not afford to buy any toys; I had to make our own toys from stick, can, board, and juice boxes. Sometimes when I look at other kids playing with their toys, such as a water gun, it was like something special. Because parents who can afford it only give their child a toy once per year, and that is on Christmas.

I never owned a bike growing up; some kids were very lucky because they had some form of relative who sometimes came from the States and worked on a farm or lived in the States. So when the work was finished or they came on a vacation to Jamaica, they could bring a bike for their loved ones. As for me, who could not afford one, first I would have to go to the garage and ask one of the mechanics for a couple of old bearings that they removed from the vehicles. Next, I got a few old tires and cut it to wrap it around the bearings; then I went to the forest and cut some sticks to make our own bike, and last we went for a test ride. The bike could only be ridden downhill because it had no pedal to pedal uphill.

Another bad thing about the homemade bike was that you might be just learning to ride, and the bike doesn't have any brake, or if it does have a brake, it might not be working properly. Otherwise, we just have to imagine going down the hill and wanting to stop but we can't stop. When you do stop, you stop the wrong way; you are in pain—your shoulder, elbow, knees, the palm of your hands—and sometimes your head gets cuts and bruises.

In spite of growing up poor, I always liked to take part in some form of sports, such as soccer and track-and-field, but I was going more toward track. When I was about eleven years old, I always ran to anywhere I am going that's close in the community. As a result of that, everyone in my little surrounding wanted me to do their little messenger work; I even ran to school. In addition to that, one day I decided to take my track more seriously, so I started to compete with the other children at my school. The schools usually have an annual competition; however, I became one of the school's best athletes.

Therefore it is easy for any child in Jamaica to become a sprint champion. For instance, I did not have a lot of transportation to choose from or I never owned a bike so I could move around as I would liked. So I had to walk or run to reach where I want to go; I could do five or more miles in a short period of time. As a result of that, anyone can become a very good sprinter. Because I was so fast in running, one day at school—I was on my lunch break, and I was playing a game called police-and-thief with some other friends—as a result of my speed, the other kids did not want me to play the role of the police because he always carried a long piece of stick and chased the ones who are the thieves. And any thief the police caught got hit with the stick. So once I was the police, they knew that somebody was going to get hit no matter what happened.

While I was playing at school one day, I was running around one of the school buildings, and another boy was running toward me from the opposite end of the school building. His name is Fitzroy Williams. He wasn't coming with a lot of speed, but I was going like a runaway train. As a consequence, we hit each other head-on; after we hit heads, I was so shaken up. Next I started to get dizzy; then I ran over to the side and sat on one of the school chairs with my hands covering my face, my head in my lap. As soon as I sat down, I felt something warm dripping in the palm of my hands. I heard a voice from a student, saying, "He is bleeding." As soon as I heard that, I forced to open my eye, but I could not because there was too much blood. My left eye was covered with blood.

Later that afternoon, a couple of older boys took me to the principal's office, and he was able to stop the bleeding very quickly since the community did not have any paramedic or any ambulance. On the other hand, the sun was very hot; it was about seventy degrees. As I mentioned earlier that transportation was a problem for us, the principal asked the two older boys, along with my brother Dixie, to take me to the nearest doctor, who is in Frank field, five miles away. We had to walk all five miles to get to Frank field. When we got to Frank field, the doctor wasn't working that day. While I was still in Frank field, my older sister, Eva, heard the news and came to see me.

She told the boys and my brother that they can leave, and she will take care of the rest. Eva and I took a taxi from Frank field to another little town by the name of Spalding, which is another five miles away from Frank field. As we reached Spalding, we went straight to the Percy Junior Hospital. Even though we were at a hospital, still the emergency room was closed for the day. Although the emergency room was closed, one of the nurses was able to clean the wound and put some new bandage on it. The next day, my sister took me back to the hospital; this time, the emergency room was open, and I was able to see a doctor. The cut was very deep they had to stitch it up; I ended up getting five stitches over my left eyebrow. When my dad finally got the news, he remarked that he did not send me to school to play.

In spite of me getting that cut, after it healed, I still wanted to continue with my track, but I could not get any help. I was to go and compete with some other school at a well-known high school in Jamaica by the name of Vere Technical. I could not afford simple shorts. My mom could not buy me a pair, and sometimes I don't like to ask my dad for anything. If I did ask him for something, he didn't answer me, so I didn't know if I was going to get it or not. Nevertheless I went and asked him for some money to buy a pair of shorts; he looked at me and asked me if I can run. I went to my grandmother's house and told her what was going on with me; she wasn't in the position to help me either, but she was thinking of making me a pair from one of her old dresses using her hands. She had a sewing machine, but it wasn't working.

However, I did not get the chance to go and compete with the other school because I did not have the gears I needed for the sport. Instead, I used whatever resource I had to go out in the morning, on the weekend, and on some mornings before I go to school; I wore regular pants to go and practice. Me and some other friends would get up at 5:00 am and run about five miles to and from. We did not have any gym to go to and workout, so we had to do our own little exercise. At 5:00 am, it is still dark, and there is not enough light on the street. The lights are about a mile apart from one another, and also the roads are not the best—there is no asphalt on it and with lots of potholes. The holes are so huge you can put a five-year-old kid in it and still have room around.

It was track time at my school again, and I still wanted to continue with my running. So one evening after school was out, all the kids who were on the school track team gathered outside for training. I had only one pair of shoes that I wear to church on Sundays and maybe the first day of the school year, which is September. But today, my mom was not at home; she went to wash some clothes for someone in the community. I took the only pair of shoes that I had and wore it to school; it wasn't in too much of a good shape because the right foot was showing my big toe through a tear on the side. Yet I still wore it to school in spite of that because it was the only pair I had. Before I started practicing, I took off the shoes so that it would not get any more damage. After practice, when it was time for me to go home and while I was getting my stuff together, I realized that my shoes were missing from where I put it down. I guess someone threw it away because it was so raggedy looking.

Although my shoes were raggedy, losing it was not good for me because now I don't have any shoes, and I was going to get a whipping from my mom when I got home. I reached home, and my mom was at home already. There I was standing outside the gate, scared to enter the house as a result of me not having the shoes that I had when I left the house in the morning. As I stood outside, there were a lot of things on my mind, for example, how I was going to tell my mom about what happened to my shoes, what I was going to eat for dinner, was I going to school tomorrow, where was the next pair of shoes coming from. In spite of the shoes missing, I still had to go and cut wood to make fire to cook food, and I also had to carry water from half a mile away for us to drink and take a shower. Therefore I just had to play man-up and take my whipping, knowing that I was wrong in the first place to wear the shoes to school without my mom's permission.

My school went on a field trip, but I did not go due to financial issues. They went to a couple of places, such as the Red Stripe beer production plant and a shoe factory that only makes shoes called Gater. During that time, Gater was the name of the brand of shoes for poor people, but still a lot of people could not afford to buy a pair for their child. The manager had given the principal of my school a few pairs of shoes. But God had always been on my side when I was growing up I was outside playing as usual (running) when I came across a door key lying in the grass. I did not know whom it belonged to, but I picked it up and put it in my pocket.

The following morning, I was in devotion at my school, and as the devotion was about to finish, Mr. Howell, the principal, said that he had an announcement to make. The announcement was that there was a lost key that belonged to the school, and if anyone found and returned it, he/she will get a reward. Even though I found a key, I wasn't sure if it was the same key he was talking about, so I held on to the key for a while. When it was break time, I asked an older boy I knew very well to follow me to the principal's office because I was a bit scared to go by myself. One reason why I was scared was that my principal doesn't stand for rubbish; he always tried his best to make sure everyone followed the right path.

As soon as I pulled that key out of my pocket, I knew that this was going to be the best day of my life. He started hugging me, he picked me up, he shared his breakfast with me, and he also asked me who my parents were. I told him my mother's name. That even made things better because my mom washed clothes for him and watched his two kids. He did not hesitate; he opened a bag and gave me one pair of the Gater shoes that he got from the shoe factory. He told me the key was the main key for the school that was lost by one of the teachers or students. I lost one pair and felt bad within myself, yet I was thankful for getting back another pair.

However, I was so happy to be in this position; I did not stay at school for the remainder of the day. I took the shoes and ran home to my mom so she can look at it. I really don't have anything bad to say about Mr. Howell. All I can say is that he was very strict; he carried a piece of leather belt in his pocket. If he saw you doing something wrong, he would call you out by your name. If he didn't remember your name, he would say, "You boy, from up Ms. Jane [my mother's name], it is you I am talking to." He might give you one strike from the belt, depending on what you were doing at the time.

However, sometimes he didn't hit you; he'd just call you and give you a little shake-up. The shake-up was almost the same as getting a whipping because when he shook you, it felt like you got hit by an NFL player. Also, his voice was so strong; when he talked, the only thing you can do was cry and try not to do anything wrong again for him to come at you some more. During that time, I was thinking that he didn't like the boys of the school, but I got to understand that the reason why he was so strict on us was because he wanted to make sure that we took the privilege we can go to school and make good use of it to get a good, solid education and also become better fathers in the future.

On the other hand, whatever he did or said to us, he only did it because he loved us, and he wanted us to achieve good things in life and contribute some good things back to our community, wherever we ended up living. That way we can make this world a better place, much better than the way we first found it, yet even today, I can still picture him and hear his voice telling me that I am going to be the teacher of tomorrow's generation, so take your education now while you can. He also told us that "it is better to teach a man how to fish, than to give a man a fish every day." At the age of fourteen, I started to play soccer more and liked drawing. My mother saw the potential in my drawing but could not do anything to help nurture it because she didn't have the money to send me to an art school so that I could develop my art skills by learning the fundamentals of art. However, when my mother got some spare time, she always liked to do embroidery on homemade towels for sale.

She would go to a dressmaker she knew in the community and ask her for some of the scrap material that she was not going to use. Then she'd ask me to use carbon and paper to trace the design she wanted on to the cloth; that really helped me get my drawing practice going. After I am through with the tracing, she used needle and threads to complete the work. Nevertheless, I knew that I had the potential, but there was no form of help to get me in an art program. In spite of me not being able to get the kind of help I needed, I still held on to the goals I had in mind. I did not want to ask my father for help because most times he doesn't speak when I ask him for something. Instead most times the answer was no.

As the time was getting closer for me to graduate from junior school, I knew that help was limited for me, so I started thinking of ways how I can earn some money the honest way. The first thing that came to my mind was to go and ask Mr. Reid for some work. It was harvesttime, and he might need some help. He gave me the work, but he was concerned about me stopping school; I explained the situation I was in to him. He looked at me and shook his head. I worked on his farm for two weeks, but I wasn't comfortable because I did not want to stop school, so I had to come up with something I can do while I am still in school.

During the two weeks I was working on the farm, it was really fun because my mom and dad were there also; there was no kitchen for us to cook our lunch, no running water. We had to go to the spring to catch water coming from the ground; and when the food was ready, Winston Brown, the farm supervisor, poured out the food on leaves on the ground for us to eat. We also did not have any spoon or fork to eat with; we had to sharpen sticks and used them to pick up the food. However, some people like my mother would bring their own utensils. We all called it bush life. When eating from the leaf, sometimes the person who ate the fastest will eat more than the person who ate slowly. And it is not a wise idea to eat fast because you might choke on the food and have nothing to drink, like a soda for example. The only thing we had to drink was water from the spring and water from the food. Although she needed the money, I really did not like to see my mother working so hard on the farm just to keep the family alive.

The property was about five acres, cultivated with orange and grapefruit; we worked in groups of three. My job was to climb the tree and pick the grapefruit or orange, another person stood beneath the tree and caught the fruits, and my mother would use a bag to carry the fruits to the nearest point where it is safe for the donkey to come and take it another mile so the truck could take it to the factory. I wasn't too worried about what was going on around me at that time; my only concern was to come and work for a few weeks to get some money put aside toward buying my graduation outfit.

Now the two weeks was finished, and it was time for me to go back to school and come up with my next plan; my plan was to use some of the money that I got to buy some candy we called busta. I took the busta to school in my backpack and sell them in class when it was break time and lunchtime. The money I received from selling the busta and the money I saved from working were used to buy all the things I needed for my graduation. I was not a flashy person, so I just settled for the cheaper stuff that I needed and not what I wanted.

Going to high school

After I graduated from junior school, it was time for me to start making other preparations for the coming school year, where I will be starting high school, which would begin September of 1993. During the summer before I started high school, all the harvesting were finished at Mr. Reid's farm and school was out, so now I had to do something to get some money to buy the things I needed for school. In spite of the harvest being finished, I still had another source that could earn me some money. There was this place that had a lot of mango trees, where I could go and pick mangoes for free to sell, even though it is only available once per year, in the summer. It is a good time for us kids when mango season comes around because all the kids are at home and our parents don't have enough food for us to eat. That way we can grab a bag and go and get some mangoes to eat.

As a result of this, we don't have to think about breakfast, lunch, or dinner; you ate all you can eat there to satisfy your stomach and then bring some home for the next day. The property had so much mangoes they just kept falling off the trees when they get too ripe; also we had to be very careful when we walked underneath the tree because the mangoes that sat there caused a lot of bees to swarm on the ground. And we had no shoes on to prevent us from getting stung on our feet by the bees; however, it was a sure thing for us to get stung when it was mango season. We had no other choice but to take the sting and keep going.

During the mango season, a lot of people drove through the community, looking to buy mangoes from us. In the community, there were a lot of people trying to get buyers for their mangoes. But the people who were buying the mangoes from us didn't want to give us a reasonable price. Because of that, we had to take the road to another community, which is about fifteen to twenty miles away from home, to get mangoes sold. We had to leave home at about 5:00 am on Saturdays and get back about 3:00 pm the same day. We travel in groups, and we have to walk all those miles to and from.

It wasn't easygoing in the morning; sometimes the rain fell overnight, and the little track we had to follow was wet and slippery. You can just imagine carrying a box on your head with at least eight dozen mangoes weighing about thirty-five to forty pounds going that distance. When I got there, I took a rest and then inspected the mangoes to see which one got soft from falling over along the way because of the condition of the road. Sometimes I got a stiff neck from carrying so many loads; in spite of us walking the long journey to get here, it only got worse because we have another mile or so to walk before the mangoes sell off. Each time I sold a few mangoes, that was when the load started to get lighter.

After I finished selling, sometimes I made like fifteen Jamaican dollars or about two US dollars; sometimes I can't afford to buy lunch out of the money I make. Instead, we had to save some of the soft mangoes to eat for our lunch. The cheapest thing that I could buy out of the money was a thing called bag juice, which is made from sugar and Kool-Aid. When we buy it, we made sure that it is well frozen; that way it would serve me a long time while I walked over the hill to get back home. On my way home, I'd stop at a little grocery store and buy me some meat we called chicken back so that my mother had some meat to cook for dinner. It got the name because it came from the back part of the chicken that has no meat on it; however, that meat was turkey for a lot of Jamaican people on holidays such as Christmas day.

Nevertheless, I wasn't afraid to go into any shop on the corner and ask for some chicken back because my mother told me one thing: that it does not matter what you eat for dinner—whether it is turkey, ham, beacon, grapefruit, or ripe banana—the bottom line is that once you get a stomach full, it is just a stomach full. Selling mangoes was very good because I used the money to buy uniform, books, shoes, and other supplies for my first year in high school. Even though I was looking forward to start a new school year and a new school, I was hoping to get the chance to go to one of the more recognized high schools so that I can get the chance to excel in more than one practical area, which included mechanic, art, and agriculture science, but that did not happen. Instead, I ended up going to another school that was recently upgraded from secondary to high school. The school was in another community named James Hill, which is five miles away from home. The name of the school is Claude McKay High.

Although the school has been upgraded to high school, the courses and the teachers did not change; they remained the same. They were still doing things the secondary way, did not have a lot of practical areas, and were still using the teachers that are not properly trained to teach at the high school level. However, I believed that the school didn't make too much of a difference; it all had to do with the child—how bad he/she wanted to get a solid education. Most of the time, as a kid, I had to push myself in the right direction, where we want to go in life. I wanted to go to high school, and the only high school I got the chance to go to was about five miles away, and I had to get up early every school morning, at about 5:00 am, and get ready to leave the house by 6:00 am to reach school by 8:00 am.

That was a big challenge for me because I had to walk all those miles five days a week, morning and evening, to and from; and sometimes I left my house without eating breakfast. But one thing is for sure: my mother always had a little brown sugar somewhere in the house. Whenever time we get some money, the first thing we bought was some sugar; that's one of the most important things she always wanted to make sure we have at home. She was going to make either some lemonade or tea for us to drink and get our stomachs full. Before I left the house for school, she would go outside and pick a few leaves from the orange tree and put them in some boiling water on the fire for a few minutes. Then she would use the water to make me a cup of tea, with no milk or nothing to eat. As soon as I am through drinking my tea, I'd start my journey to school.

During my second year of high school, I was absent from school for two weeks because I did too much walking my knees got swollen. Also, I had to keep going to the shoe repairman; the shoes, even with good care, only served me for about five months. The shoe bottom always wore down because of the walking. It was harder for me going to the high school because I had only two hours to complete five miles to reach school in the morning. Most of the time, I was so hungry and tired I reached school when the first session was finished. Although I reached school, I don't have any money to buy lunch; still that did not stop me from going to school.

Whether I did reach school early or not, I had to stay outside awhile, get rid of the sweating, and cool down before I entered the classroom. In spite of me going to school without lunch, after school I had to hurry to reach home before it gets dark so that I can do my homework and other stuff around the house, such as catching water for my mom to cook and for me to take a shower. The reason why I had to make sure that I did all my duties before it got dark was that we had no electricity at home. However, at times when I really feel bored because I didn't have any form of game such as Game Boy, Nintendo, or Xbox, I'd always think of something to make to play with. One of my favorite and the easiest toy I liked to make was one made from a piece of stick, the cover from a toothpaste, a rubber band, and the reel that the thread came with. Growing up, I did not know anything about Santa; I couldn't remember owning two toys during my childhood.

At the age of seventeen, it was getting closer for me to graduate from high school; I had one more year left. While I was in high school, I did specialize in agriculture because that was the best area the school had to offer me at that time, and working in field already, I might as well go ahead and do it. Even though I had one more year in high school, I thought now was the best time for me to start making preparations to get some money to put toward my next graduation. I went and visited my father one weekend; his new wife went and visited some other older kids he had with some other lady before he met my mom. Their names are Sharon, June, and Winsome. However, my dad told me that my sisters wanted to meet me, so the following week, my stepmother and I went and visited them. They were happy to see me; they were asking me if my father was taking care of me and if I was going to school.

They told me that I can come and spend holidays with them whenever I was ready. The first holiday coming up was summer, so I wrote June a letter, asking her if I can come and spend the holiday with them. She replied back and said that it was OK for me to come. While I was there with them on that long summer break, I usually went with the older sister, Sharon, to the grocery store. Rather than stay at home in the daytime, I thought it would be a good idea to go and ask the store manager if he need any help, which most business places needed when holidays came. I asked the first supervisor I saw on the floor, and God was on my side. She called someone from downstairs and asked if he needed some help on weekends; the person said yes, and I got the job. I started to work the next Saturday at the discount supermarket/wholesale in May Pen, Clarendon.

After the summer finished, the manager at the grocery store liked the way I worked and wanted me to continue working on weekends. I went to my mom at home and told her; she was happy for me. She told me to go ahead and take the opportunity. But I didn't know where I would stay when I went to work in May Pen. The only place I could think about was with my sisters, so I went and asked them if I could stay there on the weekends to go and work at the grocery store, to get some money to help with my upcoming graduation. They said yes. So every Friday morning, I would walk to school, carrying a bag with yam, banana, and oranges, along with my backpack, to take to my sisters' house after school in the evening.

When school finished on Friday, I would pick up the bag from a shop near the school, where I left it in the morning, and go straight to my sisters' house. As soon as they saw me coming toward the gate, they would say, "Look at the countryman coming." They believed that they are from the town because they lived in May Pen, and that's the capital for Clarendon. But still I did not like the way they said it; it made me feel like they were separating themselves from me. In spite of what they had to say to me or about me, I stayed there and went to work on Saturdays and Sundays for a while. Then I found out that I had an uncle by my mom's side of the family living close to my sister. Eventually, I found his house and started to visit him. He was living in England, but he got sickly and decided to come home. My uncle and his wife are Seventh-day Adventists while my sisters are with church of God.

Every Monday, I caught the bus in May Pen at about 5:00 am to a community called Trout Hall, and then I caught another taxi to James Hill. Everything was just working for me because while I was working at the grocery store, we had a shortage of sugar in the country, but I was able to get sugar to buy because I worked there. So I took advantage of that and made sure that I bought at least four pounds of sugar every Monday when I came home. After a long weekend of work, I had to walk the long five-mile journey after school to reach home.

This time, the money I saved up from working at the grocery store I used to buy a piglet for fifteen hundred Jamaican dollars, which was about fifteen US dollars at that time. After school, I tried to get home early so that I can go and look for a special bush that the pig ate and gave it the bush. Also, I asked my neighbors who didn't have any pig for all the waste food they had. Living in the country and rearing an animal was a little easier when it came to feeding because I didn't have to give the pig the feed that I bought at the store in the morning. Sometimes I only gave it some—one time, and that was in the evening.

Although I went through a lot of ups and downs trying to stay in high school, I have to give my father a lot of credit because even though he did not intend to send me to the school I wanted to go, he still tried his best to send me to Claude McKay; he paid the school fee for the three years I was there. So I really had to show some appreciation to him. However, my father's new wife had a daughter when he met her. Although I was a year older than her, we went to the same junior and high school. Before we got enrolled in the high school, we had to take a placement test, in order for us to get accepted in the school. Anyway, I went and took my test.

When it was time for me to go and get the result, I wasn't able to go, so my stepmother went and collected her daughter's result along with mine. I was at my father's house when she got back from the school; the first thing she said to me was, "All you boys from John's Hall are not smart because only the girls passed their exams." I went and asked another boy in the community who took the test and also went to pick up the result. He told me that one lady in the office told him that the test scores were posted at two different locations. My stepmother went to only one location for the result. However, my stepmother's remarks were that I was worthless and I must go and learn how to make furniture at a furniture shop in the community. So it might be what made my daddy feel like he didn't want to spend any money to send me to a better school; as a consequence of that, I did get the result and I did pass the test.

Instead, my stepmother's daughter was the one who was living all the luxury in life because she was living with my father; she took a taxi to school every day while I had to walk. Sometimes while I can only afford to buy a bag juice and bread with some butter on it, she was eating fried chicken and chips. She always behaved as if she was smarter than me. Although she was pretending to be smarter than me, during the time for me to graduate, I took the final exam and passed it, still coming eighth in my class of thirty-two students. She, instead, came eighteenth in the class. Up to this point, we were both in the same class.

The pig got very big, so I had to sell it to a butcher that came through the community every Friday and sold pork to the people in the community. I used the money from the sale of the pig along with the money I got from working to buy another piglet and the things I needed for my graduation. I was so unlucky that even the graduation picture I paid the school to take for me went missing; everyone got their picture except me. I asked the principal what went wrong; he told me that I have to go and ask the photographer about it. When I contacted the photographer, he told me that he gave the school all the pictures he got paid to take. Still I never got to see what my high school graduation picture looked like.

GOING TO EBONY PARK

In spite of the misunderstanding with my picture, I was happy that I graduated from high school and was looking forward to going to an agriculture school in May Pen. I graduated from high school in June 1996, when I was eighteen years old; I then started attending the agriculture school in September 1996. The name of the school is Ebony Park HEART N/TA. Even though I was going to a new school, I still was able to hold on to my job at the grocery store. It was easier for me because the store and the school were in May Pen; on the other hand, I still needed somewhere to stop on weekends, although my sisters said it was OK for me to stop by when I was going to high school and even though I was living on the school property. The next thing was that I was not sure if I'd get the weekends off. But whatever the circumstances, I knew I just had to hang in there and grind it out. Because my mother always said, "After a storm, there is calm."

My first day at this new school was really difficult for me because this was my first time leaving my parents' home to go and live with other children I didn't know before. Even though I was helping my mother financially, I did not really know how hard it was to stand on your own two feet. It was not only to stand because you have two feet, but you have to make the right decision and make it very quickly. When you are out there by yourself as a teenager with no family member close to you, there are so many things out there that can get you distracted from your goal that you have planned ahead of you.

When I got to the school, there was this big metal gate, with some security officers standing on the inside. I was so scared because the taxi that brought me there had left already, and here I was standing with a big traveling bag, packed with stuff that I was going to use, such as bath soap, tissue, books, cup, plate, fork, spoon, clothes, and cover for my bed. I left my bag in the school auditorium; we had an orientation where a lady came and took us on a tour of the school property. The tour was short because the property was very small, except for the farm, which I did not visit as yet.

After the tour had finished, which took about one hour, it was time for me to take my bag to the dorm room I was assigned to. My dorm room number is 7; I can stay at the security checkpoint at the front gate and look straight across the lawn into dorm 7. As soon as I entered the dorm, I got this feeling that this was not home. I started looking around the dorm; all I could see were sixteen bunk beds, eight on each side, and two lockers between each bunk bed. That meant sixteen people were assigned to one dorm and one person to a bed; that was when I really wanted to go back home. Over in one corner of the dorm, I saw a bottom bed with no cover on it; that was a good indication for me, that there was no one assigned to that bed as yet.

However, I walked over very gently and put my bag on top of the bed so that if someone should come after me, they'd notice that the bed was already taken. I went back outside to get some fresh air and relax my mind; I stood on the lawn in front of the dorm, looking toward the main gate, watching the taxi dropping off students who were coming for the first time and students who are returning. The first thing that came to my mind was when I was going to finish school here; next thing I knew, I noticed that I started crying, which I really could not help. So I just let it out and got it over with. Even if it was 4:00 pm in the evening, I knew that I would be at home or close to home coming from my old school; if I was at home, I would be looking forward to getting something to eat. On the other hand, I would be the one taking something home whether it was money or food so that we all can have something to eat on a Monday evening, from me working on the weekend.

My biggest concern wasn't me here at this new school but was the fact that I was the one who helped out my mother financially most of the time, making sure that food was always on the table. Now I didn't know how they were going to survive without me there for them. As the evening went by and the rest of people that lived in the dorm started coming back from the class and farm, I started to meet new people and felt a little bit comfortable and relaxed. Living in a new environment with so many people for the first time, I didn't know what to expect from them. All sixteen of us living in the dorm came from different backgrounds and traditions; even though we were all from the same country of birth, we thought differently, we talked a bit different, we looked different, and it went on and on.

Nevertheless at the end of the day, I just had to show respect to everyone, do good, stay out of trouble, and hope for the best. I started talking to some of the guys who seemed to be cool, such as Oniel Williams (otherwise known as Texas), Kurt Thompson, and Selvin Blake. Oniel is from St. Thomas in Jamaica; he played soccer and took part in track-and-field. At about 6:00 pm, I heard a loud alarm went off; I didn't know what to do. In fact, it was my first time hearing something like that so loud; anyway I didn't panic. The first thing I did was to look around me to see how the other people reacted toward the alarm. I saw my other dorm mates with their plates going toward the break room, so that was when I realized that it was the alarm that told us when the food was ready. I went to get my plate and joined the line for dinner. When it was my time to receive the food, I had to put the plate on a metal counter and wait for someone who worked in the kitchen to fix my plate. After I ate my dinner and relaxed a little, I went on to take a shower.

The shower was not one of the best, but it was still better than the one we had at home; when I was at home and wanted to take a shower, I had to go to a nearby river or catch some water in a big pan and take a bath outside. I did not have a regular bathroom with water running from a pipe, not to mention hot water. However, this bathroom at this school had a pipe that connected to the overhead shower, but there was no shower curtain. If it did have one, it was full of mildew. There was nowhere to put my soap; on the floor inside the shower, I had to put a piece of concrete brick so that I can stand on it. The reason why I had to stand on the block was that, first, there were some plumbing issues going on with the hole that let the waste water out. The water kept rising up to ankle height. Next, I did not want to catch any form of ringworm on my feet. Nevertheless I took my so-called shower.

The food wasn't the best, but at least I knew that an alarm was going to sound some time whatsoever for me to get something to eat. It wasn't a lot of food, but still I'd surely eat some dinner. It started to get dark, and as I mentioned before, I didn't know what to expect here. However, I knew one thing for sure: everyone who went to a new school here in Jamaica always got a little grubbing from the senior students. So I knew something was coming sooner or later, especially to me because I was a quiet and easygoing person. Even when I was in line for food, some of the senior students just cut right in front of me; they didn't join the line from the back.

At 9:00 pm every night, the light turned off; the security guards on campus had a main switch at the front gate, which was the main entrance to the school property. The switch controlled all the lights along the corridor and walkways. Whatever you are doing, when it reached nine, it had to stop because the light was going to be turned off. So in that case, I would have to make sure that I do all the assignments I had to turn in the next day early in the evening. Although I did not have any electricity at home, I had the privilege to use it here at this school, but at the same time, I was limited to use it. Sometimes we all tried to stay over a little after nine, but the security who was doing the patrol will come and tell us to turn the lights off. The switch for the light in the dorms was inside the dorm, so we had to turn it off.

When I was a rookie at Ebony Park, sometimes I wished that there were no nights to come; it was just like on the street when it got dark.

That was when all the bad people started coming out and the bad things happened. But the difference between here and the street was that most of the spot where the students hang out, such as the corridor, snack shop, lunchroom, and phone booth, all closed at 9:00 pm, and all saw darkness. While on the street, some light was placed throughout the night for you to see what you are doing or who is coming too toward you, even though the light wasn't close to one another.

My first night on campus was a bit scary for me because at some point, I knew that somebody was going to try some trick on me. After a long day, it was time for me to take a nap. I put on the cover for my bed and pillow; then I lay down on the bed on my back, looking up at the basement of the other person's bed, which was on the top bunk bed. I was very lucky to get a bed at the bottom; I didn't have the hassle of climbing up to the top when I wanted to sleep or sit down. In contrast to me having the bottom bed, it also had an advantage and a disadvantage. The advantage for me was that I can sit on my bed any time or even take a quick nap on my lunch break. On the other hand, the disadvantage was that the other person on the top bed doesn't have anywhere to sit down, so the first place they think of sitting is on your bed, especially when they are just coming from the farm.

I surely did not know what time I fell asleep, but I knew one thing for sure—that the same alarm that told me when the food was ready was the same one that woke me at 5:00 am the next day, for me to catch the truck that would take me to the farm for the first time. As soon as the alarm went off that morning, I jumped up and tried to get off my bed only to find my two feet tied together. I untied them, grabbed my toothbrush and toothpaste, rushed to the bathroom, and turned the pipe on, ready to brush my teeth. I took a look in the mirror; my face was full of shoe polish. I was not even a bit surprised; I just got my face cleaned and hurried so that the truck doesn't leave me or else I would have to walk to the farm. Although walking was not a problem for me, I didn't know where to go, and I also didn't want to be late on my first day on the farm. It took us about ten minutes to reach the farm.

In spite of the school being mainly an agriculture school, they still offered other classes such as cooking and garment construction. Everybody did not get up to catch the truck because others specialized in different areas. The farm was really larger than I expected it to be. It was approximately fifty acres of land, with both crops and livestock. For me to obtain a certificate in agriculture, I would have to do both crops and livestock. But I had a choice which one I wanted to do first; I chose livestock first because I did more livestock in high school, such as poultry rearing. Also, I just recently finished raising a pig for myself at my mom's house, so that gave me a lot of confidence. On the farm, I had to cut grass for the goats, wash at least twenty pigpens, feed one thousand broiler birds, and then milk about fifteen cows. In spite of all that work, it wasn't that hard because we worked in groups.

The teacher on the farm assigned five people to one group; each group was assigned to different areas such as piggery, poultry, and dairy. I always liked to take care of animals, mainly the young ones since they were easier to handle. At times when I had to deal with the bigger ones, like a bull weighing eighteen hundred pounds, it was not easy, especially when it is hungry or needs some water to drink. They constantly ran away from me or after me, trying to buck or kick. I remembered this one cow; her number is 33, so we called her 33. One morning, I was getting ready to milk her, but before I attempted to milk her, I had to make sure that she was properly restrained because she was the main of all the cows who liked to kick. While I was trying to put her in the sanction, she did not want to move, so I used a piece of stick to hit her on her back leg. Eventually she moved.

Even though I restrained her, she managed to graze a kick across my forehead as soon as I bent down to start milking her. It didn't hurt because when I saw her start shuffling her feet, I knew that she was getting ready to kick, so I pulled away from her. That was the reason why the kick did not connect. We finished feeding all the animals on the farm at about 7:45 am every day, and the truck would come and pick us up at about 8:00 am so that we can go to the dorm, eat breakfast, and get ready for class. However, sometimes when I got to the break room, they were finished serving breakfast; my first week was just a learning process for me. I was talking to my friend Oniel; he told me that sometimes when he left the farm and got to the break room, they stopped serving breakfast, so it was good to have a little snack stocked in my locker so if that should happen to me, I'd have something to eat.

Another thing he told me to do was to check my bed every time before I lay down to make sure that all the boards are there in the bottom of the bed. He told me that most times, the other senior students took out the board from the rookie beds so that when he came to lie down, he fell through the bed onto the other person on the bottom bed or on the floor. I could tell from experience that living in a dorm with fifteen other people was not easy; just imagine fifteen people doing fifteen different things at the same time, for example, the first person talking to another roommate, the second person shouting to somebody across the lawn, the third person listening to the radio, then another two or three people playing dominoes or card, and finally another person cooking on a hot plate.

There were so many things that went on inside the dorm; it made studying very hard, but that was one way to get me tough and ready for the real world to come. After a few months passed and I got settled in the school, new students kept coming in and students finishing their courses left the school. By the time I knew it, I became a senior, and it was time for me to return some grubbing. Yet I still did not grub anyone. Because that was not my style, I'd rather help the student in whichever way I can, whether it is in the classroom or on the farm.

While everything was running smoothly, I started working back at the grocery store on weekends, but the only bad thing was that I don't get all the weekends off; sometimes I was scheduled to work on the farm to take care of the animals. In spite of me not able to work every weekend, the school gave me 250 Jamaican dollars every two weeks, which was equivalent to 2.50 US dollars. As I received the money, the first person that came to my mind was my mother; the next day, I got an envelope from one of the nearby shops across the street from the school. Then I would write her a little letter, put the money I got inside the letter, and post it to her so that she can have some money to spend. Sometimes I don't know if she received the money or not because we both didn't have any telephone to communicate with each other; instead, I just hoped and prayed that when I did see her, she will say yes, she received the money.

When I completed my first four months at Ebony Park, I met a teacher who was a pioneer at Ebony Park. His name is Mr. Vincent Paul Myers; he had just come back from college, and he came to Ebony for a work experience, where he was assigned to my class. My class was Livestock 3B; Mr. Myers specialized in pig rearing. However, we both became good friends; whenever he was giving the class a quiz, he would ask me,

"Wilfred, are you ready?" and I would reply by saying, "Yes, sir." We always competed against each other; I studied real hard for the quiz because I wanted to score a 100 percent on the quiz, and he checked everything to make sure that all the words were spelled correctly, all Is are dotted and all Ts are crossed. One day, I did a quiz and was confident that I scored a 100 percent on the quiz. When he came to class the next day, he was just smiling. He started handing out the quiz paper that he marked; when he reached the desk where I was sitting, he started laughing more. That was when I realized that he got me on this quiz. When he gave me my paper, the score was 99 percent, I lost one point for leaving off the letter s from a word, and that's the closest I ever came to a hundred in his class.

Even though I did not score a 100 percent on any of my quiz, he still saw the hard work that I put into my classwork; he saw that I have the potential to move on to higher learning, which was the agriculture college that he had just finished studying at. He told me that he was taking some papers back to the college, and while he was there, he was going to try and get some application form from the college for the school, and he was going to make sure that I got one of the application forms. I did get one of the form; I filled it out and gave it back to him. He took all the applications back to the college. About one month later, I got a message from the college saying that my application has been accepted by the college. Everything happened so fast because I completed seven months in this present school, and now I am here getting ready to go to college. I know that this was a very big challenge for me because I did not go to a good high school in the first place.

Nevertheless I planned to give it my best shot. Although I was accepted in the college, I had to start college in August instead of September 1997. Normally I would start September, but because I did not take the subject I needed to take in high school for me to go straight to a college, instead I had to do the precollege course that took place in the summer before the September school year started. During high school, I only took the courses that gave me the credit to graduate with a school-leaving certificate or equivalent. Those subjects that I took in high school were free, so I took them because I didn't have the money to pay for the others.

As time went by, it seemed as if things were getting harder and harder on my side. Because I was getting older, there were a lot of things I would like to do, also things that I needed, mainly clothes. But I still had to give

God the glory for giving me health and strength to take me through day by day. I discovered, while growing up as a kid, that when I passed one stage in life, the next stage coming up was always better than the previous stage, and it also prepared me for the future.

Whatever I did at Ebony Park wasn't too much of a difference from what I was doing while growing up as a young kid going to school. Although sometimes I really thought about those days in the past and compared them with what I am doing at this point in time, for example, writing this page, I had electricity to see what I am writing now, but back in those days, if I wanted to do my homework, I would have to do it early in the evening before nighttime. Otherwise I had only one source of light to rely on, and that was the glass lamp. The lamp had a glass shade on it that was made from a very thin type of glass; the top of the shade had a cylinder-looking shape while the bottom had a sphere-looking shape. Also on the shade was this signature writing Home Sweet Home.

The lamp used kerosene oil in order for it to light up, but having one light in the house was sometimes not enough for everyone to see using it. Instead, I'd make my own lamp with any regular glass bottle, mostly the old glass bottle that Pepsi usually came in. First, I poured some kerosene oil into the bottle. Second, I rolled some old newspaper into a cylindrical shape that will fit into the mouth of the bottle. Third, I inserted the newspaper into the bottle's mouth tightly; then I shake the bottle so that the kerosene oil soaked through the paper properly. Finally, I lighted the paper using matches. After I made my light, it was time for it to be used, so I put the bottle in the middle of the room, whether it was on a table or on the floor. Most of the time, it's on the floor so that everybody who needed the light for homework can gather around the light and use it. But somebody had to keep shaking the bottle every fifteen minutes so that the paper was kept wet with the kerosene oil.

Because the light is limited, I had the tendency of getting closer to the light so that I can see; sometimes I get too close to the light. The fire from the lamp started burning the hair on my eyebrow and my head; when I used this type of light, anybody on the street or at school can tell because it always left the inside of my nose black from the smoke that the lamp gave off. Also, if anyone in the house had any white clothes, it also got black spots and the smell of kerosene oil.

Going to agriculture college case

The time had come for me to start the precollege course, and I didn't see the first dollar to pay for my school fee. I really didn't know what first move to make, but the first person that came to my mind was my father. However, I did not feel comfortable to go and ask him for the money. Because I was older and he had younger kids that needed the money for school, so I thought it was time for me to launch out more on my own. I was like a person who will tell you the truth and nothing else but the truth. Regardless of what my stepmother might say or do, I still had to give her a lot of credit because when I asked my father for something and he didn't answer, my stepmother was the one who followed through and made sure that I got some positive results.

Even though I didn't feel like asking him for the money, I had to play man up and put all those negative thoughts behind me and went and asked him for the money—I knew that he didn't like to talk, yet he was a good listener. He did not say whether he was going to give or not, he just listened to what I had to say and then left for the field in the backyard. I didn't want to wait for him to get back, so I left, but the good thing was that I did not wait until the last minute to ask him for the money. So that way, whenever he made up his mind, I still had time to make the necessary adjustment I needed, such as asking some other family members or friend. Before, when I need something, I usually told my stepmother what I needed, and then she will ask him for it. He normally did the same thing to her, but at the end of the day, he will give her the money to buy whatever I need, if I really need it.

The school fee was US $200; however, he finally gave me the money, but it took him a long while to give it to me. At that time, I was close to twenty years old, and I really decided that this was the last time I was asking my parents for anything, no matter how small it was. After all that I went through to get the money for school, there was still another obstacle in the way. This time, I had a limited number of clothes, no money in my pocket to spend, and only had one pair of shoes. Before I was accepted in the college, I always talked to Mr. Myers about my childhood life; the day when I was leaving Ebony Park for college, Mr. Myers drove me and some other student in one of Ebony's transportation to the college in another city by the name of Portland in Jamaica.

Going to this new college was more challenging because it was farther away from home and my family than Ebony Park was. But Mr. Myers was like a big brother to me because he made sure that I got someone good that he knew during his final year at the college for my roommate. The roommate that I had was Jermaine Hunter. This was Jermaine's second time taking the precollege course. He took it the first time but did not pass it, so he came back to take another shot at it. So Mr. Myers made sure we both stayed in the same room because of Jermaine's college experience. The precollege courses were very compact because normally the course should last for one year, but this time around, the college reduced the time from one year to three months, from June to August. So I knew that it was going to be a hard three months for me, more so because I did not go to a good high school in the first place and was not able to take the courses that will get me ready for college. At the college, there were more older students than what I was expected, and that alone got me a little scared as a rookie. It was on a Sunday when we got to the college. Everyone was just trying to pack away their things and get situated, but for me, I did not have a lot of things to put away in the first place. I just put my bedcover and pillowcase on and put my bag on top of my bed, and then I went outside and walked around the college ground for a little while. The next day, Monday, we had an orientation, and some of the members of the school board came and spoke to us. The main thing that they put a lot of emphasis on was that "every new student must respect their senior."

With that said by the school board, every move I made, there was a senior student somewhere watching for me to do something wrong. Sometimes I didn't have to do anything wrong, but they still used what the school board said to their advantage. For instance, one evening I was going to the break room for dinner, when I was about five steps away from the break room, there was this guy sitting on a chair outside of the break room, facing the direction that I was coming from, he called me over. The only way to reach him was to walk though the lawn. As soon as I got over to him, he said to me, "Grub, man, you don't know that you are not allowed to walk on the lawn?" I told him, "I didn't know that I am not allowed to walk on the lawn, and furthermore, you are the one who called me over." He told me to go back around and walk on the concrete pavement.

The next thing that happened to me was on another morning. While I was coming in from the farm, I was running late for class. I was living on the third floor of the dormitory, but I got lost and ended up on the second floor, where the entire final-year students lived. There was this group of students standing in the hallway. As quickly as they saw me, they knew that I didn't live on this floor; they asked me what I was doing on this floor. I told them that I got lost trying to find my room. They told me, "It's OK, but don't let it happen again." However, since I was there already, they were going to have me make up all the beds on the second floor. After I finished making up all those beds, I was extra late for class.

Even when I was doing my laundry, some senior boys would just bring their clothes over and pour it out on me and tell me to "keep washing, grub man." They'd also take all the spoiled produce from the farm in the evening to throw at us when it got nighttime, for example, ripe breadfruit, spoiled eggs, pig feces, and even their own urine. But Jermaine and I normally walked together during the night, so we looked out for each other. We still had fun regardless of what happened on campus; we played soccer with some other friends in the evening after class, and we also had our own little study group after we finished playing soccer.

On the other hand, sometimes after we finished studying, we got very hungry, so Jermaine and I came up with an idea for us to go on the farm in the evening after dinner, before it got dark. We would climb the coconut tree and pick a few coconut; we then cut the coconut and pour the water out into an igloo so that we can have it to drink at night when we get hungry, because we didn't have money to buy snacks to eat at night.

In spite of me and Jermaine being always together most of the time, it came one weekend when he went home to visit his family. I did not have the money to take the bus home, so I decided to stay on campus that weekend. Sunday night of that weekend, I was in my room studying.

I started to get hungry, but I didn't have any money to buy something to eat, and Jermaine was not there. So I needed to think of something on my own to stop this hunger. I didn't really want to go to the farm by myself because it was night already and I didn't have any light to see with. Anyway, I remembered seeing some orange trees at the front of the farm near the college parking lot; it was so dark. Even if someone was wearing a white suit, I still could not see that person.

I managed to find the orange trees in the dark; I fell several of the oranges on the trees until I found the ones that are ripe and picked a few to take back to my room to eat that night. The following week, Mr. Myers came to the college to check on us to make sure we were OK; he also brought us a bag with snacks. As for me, he brought a couple of T-shirts because he saw that I was in need of them. At that time, I only had three pairs of pants and three shirts, with all the struggles that I was going through at this college, trying to pass the precollege course. One day, I was in my room when somebody at the phone booth called me and told me that somebody on the line wanted to talk to me. I wasn't expecting any phone call from anyone. Moreover there is only one phone box on the school campus, and that was where most of the senior boys hung out. And they also joked when it came to people getting phone calls; sometimes persons who were expecting phone calls had to stay by the phone to hear it when it rang, because it is out in the open and that made it very difficult and hard to hear.

However, I went to see if someone was really on the line and wanted to talk to me. As a matter of fact, the person should be gone by then because I took so long to get the phone. In spite of me taking so long, someone was there for real; it was my stepmother. At least somebody remembered me. I was happy at first, hoping to hear some good news such as she was coming to see me next weekend or she sent some money in the post office. Instead, she called to tell me that with the money that my father gave to me, I must make sure that I passed the precollege course because my younger sister Shernette, her daughter, needed the money to go to Edwin Allen High School in Frank field.

My head was already messed up because I was thinking about the year 2000—how the world was going to end, and that was when my three-year course would finish. Also, the year 2000 was going to catch me at college, away from my mother. As a result of what she told me over the phone about the money, I lost focus on my college work immediately, and that was when everything about college started to deteriorate. The next thing I knew, I failed the math and chemistry exams. It was a must for me to pass all the courses in order for me to be accepted into the college, for the school year that would start on September 1997.

Even though I did not pass the precollege course, I felt like I just finished in one of those top high schools in the country; my plan was to work part-time and go back to school and retake those classes that I had failed. As soon as I got all my stuff packed together, I left the college and went to my mom's house. At first, I really felt bad within myself and also very disappointed, but I tried very hard to leave the past and the entire negative thoughts behind me and move forward and live. But I still didn't like failing, so whatever goals I set in life, either long-term or short-term, I did my best to accomplish them most of the time.

Working a Full-Time Job

Although I was working at the grocery store on and off because of me going to school, I went back one more time and asked for the job, and they were willing and able to rehire me because they knew that I was a good worker. This time I was working full-time. The way how

I was happy for the job; I did not even think about where I was going to stay or how I was going to get to work. I definitely could not live with my mother. The main reason why it would not work out was that I'd have to leave early in the morning, and there wasn't a lot of transportation on the road that early in the morning. The next alternative was to ask my sisters who live in May Pen for me to stay with them again, to work and try to take some classes in the evening after I leave work.

I did not know how to approach them, but I figured out a way how to do it. Eventually it worked out, and they said yes, that it was OK for me to stay with them. After a few months of staying with my sisters, things started changing between me and them. I would come home from work tired and hungry, hoping that one of my sisters cooked some dinner and left some for me; they cooked dinner but none was left for me. Also when I got home from work at night, I knocked on the door, but they took a long time to open the door. One night, they took so long to open the door that I decided to put two chairs together and make myself a bed and sleep. Instead, I thought about how sleeping outside can become very dangerous; then I heard my sister June come and open the door. But before I entered the house, she told me that the next time I went and visited my uncle by my mother's side of family, I must ask his wife if I can stay with them while I worked. Most Sundays, I didn't get the chance to go to church with them because I worked Monday through Saturday, so Sunday was the only day I got off. However, I would stay home and do my laundry; that way I would have some clean clothes to wear to work the coming week. My sisters would leave for church on Sundays, but they'd lock up the entire house and leave me outside with the dirty clothes and the washing pan because I did not go to church with them. I grew up in church, but at that time, I just could not make it every Sunday.

Even though I was working, I could barely find clothes to wear to work, not to mention clothes for church; moreover I just started working full-time on the job and was trying to get settled so that I could buy some clothes for church. Instead I had to say thanks to Mr. Myers again for a couple of shirts he gave me at the college. One Monday night I came home from work, June asked me what my uncle said about me staying with them. In spite of what I was going through in my sister's house, I did not take her seriously when she told me to ask my uncle's wife if I can stay with them. My sister told me that the reason why they didn't want me at their house was because my father did not take care of them, and because of that, they didn't have anyone to go to for some help. So I am not allowed to get any help from them.

That same night, I took my backpack with the few pants and shirts I had and left my sisters' house in 1997 and never returned again. I went to my uncle's house that same Monday night and asked his wife if I can stay with them for a while. She said yes, I can stay with them because they really needed some company in the house at night, but she would like to know why my sisters didn't want me at their house. I really didn't like lying, but I felt so bad within myself, knowing that some of my close family members forsake me; I told her that my sisters have some family coming from abroad who were to stay with them for a little while. About three months later, I remembered my uncle's wife asking me when my sisters' family was going back. That time, I realized it was time for me to make the next move.

One day, I was talking to one of my friends, by the name of Richard Branford, about the things that I went through at my sisters' house. He looked at me very good and told me that the only thing I could do then was to get myself one little bedroom to rent. It might sound foolish at first, but in the long run, I was going to enjoy it. I was glad for the encouragement because right away I started thinking of things that I was going to need for my room. After work, Richard and I were outside the grocery store talking; he told me that he was going to ask a lady about a one-bedroom apartment she was renting out a few weeks earlier.

The next day Richard came to work, he told me that he has some good news for me. I was so anxious to hear what the good news was all about. He told me that he got the room for me, and I can move in the next day without any down payments. I had only six thousand Jamaican dollars, which is about one hundred US dollars, at that time in a savings account. I took my lunch break the following day and went to a little furniture store on the corner to look at some beds that they have been selling; I asked the manager of the store which of the beds were on sale. He gave me a good deal on one of the beds that I liked. He sold me the bed for $5,500 Jamaican dollars.

After work, Richard and I went back to the furniture store, along with the transportation that we were going to use to take the bed to the apartment. The transportation was a car; the driver charged me three hundred Jamaican dollars. The three of us picked the bed up and put it on top of the car, and then we used a piece of rope to tie the bed firmly to the car to prevent it from moving while driving. We reached the house safely even though the road was so narrow and full of potholes. I really didn't like the area where the room was because it was in the country; and May Pen, where I was living with my sisters, was more like the city, and it was closer to the grocery store. But as Richard had told me earlier: while it might not be what I was looking for, but the bottom line was that no one can tell me when to come or when to leave. I pushed my own door at the end of the day.

He also told me that at times I was going to feel lonely by myself, but time will come when I was going to look back and ask why I didn't do this much earlier, because it was going to make me a better person. In my first evening at the new apartment, I basically didn't have anything except for the bed—no food, no curtain for the window, no bedcover, no stove to cook on, no refrigerator, and no family close by. However, I had three good things that money can't buy. First, I had the good grace of God with me. Second, I had Richard and Mr. Myers. After I got my bed together, Richard went to one of his sisters who lived about one block away from my new apartment. He then returned with a pair of window curtains for me to put at the windows. That was so cool because I had no idea where to go and get something to put at the window to stop people from looking inside the room and also to stop air from coming in at night.

Both of us left for work every day at the same time and went back home the same time, but even though I was paying my own rent and pushing my own door, there was a challenge for me to figure out. The challenge was the distance from where I live now to where my job was. The distance was about half the journey from my mom's house. Going to work wasn't the problem; the problem was getting home after the grocery store closed late at nights. The same taxi that we used to carry the bed to the apartment, we also took to get home in the evening, and sometimes in the morning. On weekends, there was no set time when we were going to leave work. Sometimes when we went to the bus stop, all the buses and taxis have stopped running. At times we get a ride, but the vehicle was only going half the journey, so we have to get off and walk the rest of the way home.

One Saturday night, we got off work at about 11:30 pm. The only taxi that was there on the stop was going to another community called Summer Field; from Summer Field, we had another three miles to walk to reach home. That was the closest the taxi would go because the taxi driver wasn't one of our regular drivers. However, the only option we had was to take a shortcut through a place called danks. On our way through the shortcut, we heard a strange sound; we stopped for a while and listened very keenly to the sound to try and see if we could figure out what was making the sound and where the sound was coming from. We could not figure the sound out, but we continued walking. While we were walking, we started smelling a funny scent. Instantly we recognized the scent: it was the muddy water from the river, and the water was making the sound.

The river had taken in water from the rain that fell in another community. The Rio Minho is the longest river in Jamaica; it runs through Frank field all the way to May Pen. Sometimes it rained very hard only in Frank field; it rained so heavy the river took in water about five feet tall from side to side. At times when I was in May Pen and happened to pass over the bridge, I saw the water looking yellow and muddy. Once I saw the water with that color and running so heavily, I knew that the rain had fallen very hard in the Frank field area. In spite of us walking home half of the journey that Saturday night, there were four of us going to the same community. We had no light whatsoever, so we can barely see where to put our feet.

We had to take our shoes off and roll our pants a foot up; the water didn't rise very high that night but still managed to reach me a little above my knee. However, the current in the water was very strong; we had to hold one another's hands and slowly cross the river. When it rained and the river took in a lot of water, it always gave off a funny scent. The scent was not a stinky scent, but it had a muddy scent, which was caused by the water washing the topsoil from the earth, which most times led to soil erosion, the tearing away of valuable topsoil. Having a river close to home can be fun at times because when Richard and I were not working, he would get a few of his friends, and we all went to the river. Some of us would take clothes to wash while the others just went for the fun to swim or to catch some fish.

Having a river close to us was like having our own beach because the real beach was miles away from us, and most of the time, we can't afford to go to a beach. On weekends, the river was the place to be because a lot of people didn't have any pipe water at home; they came to the river to do their laundry. Also, some time of the year, there was always water shortage, such as in the summer. And when it got very hot, the river was the only place I want to be rather than sit at home, in a house that had no air conditioner and no refrigerator that can give me some cool air or some water to drink. However, as I got older, I started to have a personal relationship with God; I realized that I had an inner voice that spoke to me a lot of times. The whispering voice always talked to me in a positive way; most of the time I listened to what the voice told me to do, but sometimes I ended up in a situation where I had to stop for a while and think carefully and sometimes ask myself how I can give up something that I had now for something that I couldn't see or something that I was not sure how to get. Even though I thought about it most of the time. But one day while I was on my way to work, I just started thinking of ways how I can make my life, my family, my close friends, and other people around me better. So I reached work and started working, but something kept bothering me until the voice told me to go and apply for a passport.

I surely did not hesitate; as soon as it was time for me to take my lunch break, I hurried to a travel agent's office across the street from my job, by the name of B J's, travel agent and picked up a passport form. In a couple of days, I gathered all the documents required for the passport; I then took them to the agency along with the fee for processing. They did all the paperwork and told me that it would be ready in three weeks' time. At the end of three weeks, I went back to check with them, and my passport was ready. I took my passport home with me, and I made sure that I put it up very carefully so it wouldn't get wet or damaged. Even before I got my passport, I always had the intention of traveling over to some foreign country, but England was my first priority.

Although I was still working at the grocery store, sometimes I got a feeling that it was soon time for me to move on to a higher level. But whatever happened, I still had respect for my job, regardless of what the job is, because that was what put food on my mother's table and paid my bills. I never looked down on any job as long as it was honest and accepted in the sight of God. I might not be the best employee, but I am going to get the work done; also I might not be the quickest worker, but I was going to set a pace that my body will allow me to go at and continue at that pace until I accomplished my goals.

Because of me being a good worker, one Saturday I was at my workstation trying to get the job done; my job was to parcel out some cornmeal into two-pound packages. The cornmeal comes in twenty-five-pound packages; after I finished parceling them out, I then put them on the shelf so that the customers can buy them. I was almost through doing that when my supervisor came and asked me to go and relieve an employee who worked in the meat department for lunch. The person I relieved was filling the customer's bottle with retail cooking oil; there were a lot of customers in line, waiting to get their bottle filled with cooking oil. Before I started serving the cooking oil, I had to make sure that I had enough oil in the forty-gallon container to serve from.

So I had to use a five-gallon bucket to carry the cooking oil from downstairs up, about twelve steps, before I got to the meat room upstairs and pour it into the forty-gallon container until it was full; then I could start serving. Eventually I managed to get the line down to about four people. Now the line was down at the meat room; on the other hand, the cash register line was not moving because the person who was packing the customers' grocery after it cashed ran out of bags to put the grocery in. Because of that, the counter got jammed with groceries. When it reached the month's end and all the customers who got their salary—such as teacher, nurse, doctor, and the police—came out to shop for the following month, that was when the situation got worse. And when they shopped, they bought a lot of things.

As a result of what happened at the cash register, my supervisor came to the meat room and asked me and another guy to go to the storeroom and get some bags to pack the customers' grocery in. The manager for the store knew that this time of the month was always the busiest, so they ordered extra bags and boxes for times like this. Because of the extra bags and boxes we brought back to the store, it resulted in things going back to normal. Even though I was helping out the other areas, I still had to keep an eye on my workstation to make sure that enough cornmeal was on the shelf for the customers to buy. While I was putting away the last stack of bags, my supervisor came and asked me to pack behind the cash register until the guy who worked there came back from his lunch break. So I went and did it. Although I was there packing, my body started to slow down physically due to tiredness. After the guy came back from lunch, I left and went back to my original workstation. As I reached my workstation, my supervisor came over and started shouting at me, saying, "Why is there no cornmeal on the shelf? If you don't want to work, change your clothes and come upstairs for your check now." Even though I needed the money, I surely changed my clothes and went for my check and went home.

If my body wasn't in good shape and I wasn't eating properly, there was no way I could survive in a tough job like that. Back in those days, we didn't have anything like a forklift or pallet jack. We had to do everything manually. Mondays were receiving day, when the truck would come to the back of the store with two hundred bags of flour, two hundred bags of rice, and two hundred bags of sugar, each bag weighs 100 pounds, except for the sugar that weighs 110 pounds. However, there were eight of us that worked in the weighing section. We all had to carry it until it was finished; then the next day, we had to weigh out all those bags into two-pound packages.

To begin with, I didn't have a job anymore, but God and the other employees knew that I worked very hard. Nevertheless, I knew that the day will come when I had to leave the grocery store and move on to something else, even though it was hard for me to leave my job. Instead, I was happy to stay home for a few months and get some rest before I started looking for some more work. On the other hand, when it was time to move on in life, nothing could stop it—only the power of God, and he knew what was best for me. One Sunday, I decided to start looking for a job; I went and bought a Sunday Gleaner. My intention was to look through the employment section and see who was hiring. I didn't reach too far with my search before I came across this security company by the name of Atlas Protection. Once I saw that they were hiring, I immediately stopped searching; I said to myself, I am going to give this company a try.

I knew that doing a security job was very dangerous because I had to protect, my life and other people's lives, and property. But I still wasn't too scared of the job due to me believing in God, knowing that there is a God, and with having him in my heart, in every move I moved, all things were possible. So I went to visit my uncle in May Pen the following Monday, and while I was there, I used his telephone to make a call to the security company. I spoke to the secretary; she told me what documents I needed to have in order to get the job. Then she scheduled an appointment for me to come in and take a placement test. I really wanted this job, but now I had to travel all the way to St. Ann's Bay even though I had never been there before.

The address that she gave me over the phone was straight forward; however, the easiest way for me to reach St. Ann's Bay was to catch a bus named Beverly's that leaves from May Pen and go all the way to Ocho Rios, but I would get to my stop before the bus reaches Ocho Rios. The main reason why this bus, Beverly's, was on this route was to transport the farmers with their produce, to get them to sell in St. Ann's and Ocho Rios. Where I stayed at the apartment, the distance from where the bus passes was about a fifteen-minute walking distance. I woke up very early one morning and caught the bus; it traveled through a few community such as Brandon Hills and Kelliths.

The ride on the bus wasn't one of the best. Because the bus was so long, it had made every turn wide; also, the road was very narrow. Despite the narrowness of the road, this route was also used by a lot of big rig trucks that carry sand from the Rio Minho to Ocho Rios. Because of the narrow road, the bus had to drive slowly to reduce the risk of an accident. However, while I was sitting in my seat just about to fall asleep, the bus was going around a very deep corner. I contrast a truck was coming from the opposite direction of the road. First, I heard a loud horn coming from the truck; second, our bus driver had to step on the brakes quickly just to prevent a head-to-head collision. As a result of the sudden stop that our bus driver had to make, every passenger in the bus was rocking and bowing.

The bus driver didn't just stop the bus from colliding head-on with the truck, but he also stopped the bus from going over a precipice. I was sitting on the inside seat, so I got up from my seat and took a glance through the side window of the person I was sitting beside. The bus stopped at the edge of the precipice; from what I could see, the precipice was about twenty-five to thirty feet deep. However, no one was injured, and therefore I made the trip safely. My test went through fine; I passed both the test and the interview, so now I have to go back home to pack my stuff to take to Ocho Rios for a week of classroom training.

I got back from Ocho Rios before Richard came home from work; when he got home, I told him that I got a new job. He was happy to hear that I got a new job, but on the other hand, he said that he was going to miss me as a good friend. I also went to the owner of the property where I was living and explained to her that I lost my job at the grocery store. But I got another job in Ocho Rios; however, I still want to keep the apartment here so that whenever I get a couple of days off, I can come home and have somewhere to stay. We also came to an agreement on how I was going to pay my rent.

While I was packing the things I was going to take with me to Ocho Rios, my inner voice told me to make sure that I take my passport with me because I am not coming back to live in Clarendon. So I followed the voice and took my passport with me to Ocho Rios on the same Beverly's bus again; this time, everything went smoothly. When I reached the Ocho Rios bus terminal, I got off the bus and took a taxi from the bus park to a place called Pineapple. That was where the other security office was located. After I finished at the office, one of the security supervisors took me in one of the company vehicles to the camp where I will be staying, in a community called Exchange.

When I got out of the vehicle and went inside the house that they called camp, it was nothing compared with all those boarding schools that I went to or lived in before. Instead, it was the worst living condition I ever came across. For example, no one was assigned to any bed. Approximately twenty people were living at the camp during the daytime, and by the time those twenty people left for work in the night, there were another fifteen people coming in from the day shift. Because of the overcrowding, they had more people than beds; no one made up their bed and just left it to work. If so, when you returned, someone was already sleeping in your bed.

The windows in the rooms had no curtains, the floor was dirty, the lawn outside needed cutting. There was a pool in the backyard that was not in working condition; instead it was full of stagnant water, which may lead to the breeding of mosquitoes. The entire bathroom fixture wasn't working. And all those I just talked about, I saw in just a few minutes. In spite of the living conditions on the camp, nothing was going to stop me from getting what I came here for. So I was hanging in there while I hoped and prayed for the best because I was not going to quit this early either because a quitter is a loser, and I didn't come this far to lose.

The first week of classroom training went OK even though camp life was horrible, but I still managed to pass the final test at the end of the week. On Friday, the last day of training, after everything was finished in the class room, it was time for me to get my uniform and get ready to take up duty on location for the first time in my life as a security officer. At about 7:00 pm, I had to go on location, which was my first time working at night and also my first location. It was cold and windy that night, but I had to bear it. As a rookie in the security field, I had to work with a K-9 (dog); I had to take the K-9 everywhere I went, although they taught us the nine commands the K-9 should listen to during the one week of training. But on the other hand, the most of the K-9s that the company owned weren't trained to listen to the commands.

Sometimes I would like to tie the K-9 and go to the bathroom, but because it wasn't trained properly, I didn't want to take that risk of tying the K-9, and when I returned from the bathroom, I can't get close enough to untie it due to the fact that I was new to the job. The K-9 didn't recognized me, and I didn't know the nature of the K-9, if it was aggressive or not. Most of the time, they were aggressive and likely to bite. The nine commands were very simple and straightforward; they are heel, sit, down, come, stay, leave, watch him, get him, and hold him. A well-trained K-9 should follow all these commands. However, as time went by on the job, I got to know the ins and outs of the job; I was very lucky to get a few good locations at some of the hotels in Ocho Rios. Me being a security, I had to keep my eyes open at all times. As I mentioned before, I had other people's lives that depended on me, especially the guest who came to visit the island. I was working at this hotel by the name of Ciboney at the time before Sandals bought the property and changed the name. A few security were assigned to guard the outside perimeter fence that surrounded a portion of the hotel.

The reason why a security presence must always be there, mainly at nights, was to prevent unauthorized persons from gaining entry to the property by jumping over the fence or to stop the employee from throwing things over the fence and have somebody receive it on the other side.

During daytime, there were no security guards at that location because whatever might happen there was only likely to happen at night. At night, there were about four security officers on the location—one security that carries a firearm, the other three uses a K-9 to patrol the fence, the entire area, and sometimes work at other locations during the day—for instance, working an eight-hour shift at Dunn's River Falls and then come to Ciboney in the evening to take up the regular location.

However, sometimes when I got to Ciboney in the evening, I was so tired and sleepy; sometimes I didn't get the chance to eat lunch, mainly on the days when there were three cruise ships in the port. Whenever I worked at Dun's River, most of the time I work at the main gate where all the tour buses that carry the guests from the cruise ship enter the property. Although I was working, sometimes I didn't have the money to buy lunch. It was always difficult for me when I start a new job since I had to catch up on all the bills that were behind while I was off work, yet I only get paid every two weeks.

At Ciboney, there was nowhere to take shelter except for a little great house on the way to Ciboney. It barely has any roof on the top, so what I did was stop by the supermarket and get me some old cardboard and plastic to make a little shelter, just in case it started to rain. The shift at Ciboney started at 7:00 pm, but between 7:00 pm and 7:30 pm, a supervisor would drive through to make sure that the location was covered with the right number of security officers. And then later at night, he'd make another patrol; this time to make sure everything was in order and we were OK. One evening, I went to Ciboney after I left Dunn's River Falls; this time I was really tired. After my supervisor made the first patrol, I went to sit on a big rock that was lying close to where I made my little shelter. A tree was behind the rock, so I leaned back and rested my head on the tree.

The next thing I knew was that I felt a bright light shining in my face. I jumped up so quickly, but it was just my supervisor making his patrol and seeing me sleeping. He told me that I must be more careful because someone different from him could come here and see me sleeping and hurt me. I didn't know how I went to sleep because it was dark, cold, and the mosquitoes were giving me all I could handle. I enjoy working at Ciboney because it sat on top of a hill that overlooked downtown Ocho Rios; I also got a clear shot of the ocean. At 6:00 am, I would hurry and walk to the great house to watch the cruise ship coming in to dock. Sometimes there were more than one cruise ship coming in, so I'd stay and watch them one by one. I stayed in this job for about seven months.

But things weren't working out for me because I was working seven days a week, and I had to request a day off. Even when I request for a day off, it was not sure if I was going to get off that day. It took a long time before I got one day off. However, one day wasn't enough for me to go and visit my parents in Clarendon; therefore I would rather have at least two days off, and that was hard to come by, so I had to give up the job. During the time I was thinking of leaving the job, I was sending out applications to other hotels in Ocho Rios. I was able to get a job at Shaw Park Beach Hotel, but I didn't work for long there. even though I was no longer working for Atlas Protection, I was still able to stay at the camp in exchange.

Although I didn't stay at Shaw Park Hotel very long, I was still able to get a job at another hotel; this job was at Sandals Ocho Rios Golf and Resort. I started working at Sandals in the year 2000 through 2001; I was working as a hotel security, with the hotel and not with a private company. The experience was good because I got the opportunity to work at the front of the hotel and interact with the guests and also meet different people. The hotel buys a lot of produce from the local farmers such as yams, potatoes, bell peppers, cabbages, carrots, and lettuces. However, the farmers had to come and pick up their check on Fridays at the hotel's main gate. Whichever security was working at the main gate had a procedure that must be followed each and every day; the guest who was checking in at the hotel will go to the front desk and get checked in while the farmers who are coming to pick up their checks were not allowed to park on the hotel property. The parking area was kept in reserve for the guests only. The farmers would have to find some parking on the street.

When the farmers came to the security booth, we normally treated them with respect, as if they were checking in as guests. First, I greeted them, second, we asked them for their names, third, we addressed them by their names. Then I asked, "How can I assist you today?" Most of the time, the farmer would say that he/she was there to pick up a check; after I got all the necessary information that I needed, then I called the accounting department to find out if there was a check for that person or company. If they did have a check for that individual person, I directed the person to find the accounting office and also called and informed the other security who are working in the hotel lobby that someone was coming through the lobby to the account office. Then the lobby security will ensure that the person went only to the accounting office. That way, we could prevent unauthorized persons from entering the property. Because the hotel was all-inclusive, once somebody entered the hotel, they can eat or drink whatever they wanted and they can even do other things that were harmful to the guests and the property.

While I was on duty at the main gate one Friday evening, it was very busy; a lot of farmers were coming in to pick up their checks. A gentleman came up to the booth and told me that he was there to pick up a check. I went through the whole procedure with him, but the only difference this time there were no security working in the lobby. So I had to leave my location at the front gate and walk with the man to the lobby and show him where to go and make sure that he went straight to the accounting office only. The main gate to the lobby were just a few steps away from each other. But while I was on my way back to the main gate, the man asked another man he met in the lobby, "Where is the accounting office?" The man was willing to show him where the office was.

Guess who the man he asked to show him the accounting office was—the hotel manager. His name was Michael Darby. The manager called my supervisor immediately and told him to move me from the main gate because I didn't give the man the right information and direction. It led to me getting fired. Even though I lost my job, my inner voice told me not to worry; it was "move on time" again.

Now I was back to the drawing board again, trying to figure out what my next move was. But being who I was, still staying at the camp in exchange, I saw what the guys were in need of—a little snack shop close to the camp. That way they can easily stop and get something to eat quickly rather than cook. There was this guy that I knew very well; he does carpentry work for a living. I went and asked him if he could make me a little stall that can be locked at night to sell snack to the guys at the camp. He told me yes, that he would make it for me, but I had to find the material to make it. I found all the materials and paid him to build it. After I got it built, I asked three of my friends along with myself to help carry it to the location that I wanted. The location was in front of the camp.

The guys were so happy of the stall; they were even happier than me because they didn't have to walk the long distance anymore to buy some snacks. The next day, some other friends came over to help me build some seats and a table where they can play dominoes and cards. The business was going fine because some of the guys that I knew very well would take stuff until they get paid, which was every two weeks. However, crediting was very risky because a security could get transferred to another city with the blink of an eye. And all that money would be a loss for me. But on the other hand, it would be a learning lesson: for instance, the same way I was looking for my money when payday comes, the same way it reached the month's end, those big credit card companies are looking for their money also. Everything was going very good until one day, when a security that I knew very well had a death in his family. He asked me to follow him to the wake. We both went and spent the entire night at the wake. When we returned the next morning, we discovered that the stall had been broken into; they took out a few things such as beers, cigarettes, some coins, and a scientific calculator.

It wasn't a surprise to me anyway; I was anticipating something like this to happen, or similar, because it wasn't secured enough into the ground or a permanent structure, and also there was no light there during the night. I continued doing that for a few more months, but in the meantime, I was still dropping off application forms at different employers. I was not the type of person that got intimidated easily by other persons, so I wasn't going to make anybody or anything stop me from selling my stuff at the camp until I was ready to stop. One day I was at the stall, I received a phone call from a very famous restaurant in Ocho Rios by the name of Island Grill. I went for an interview, and from there, I got the job. I started working there in 2001. At that time, I was twenty-three years old; even though it was a new experience for me, I was ready to take on a new challenge because my inner voice told me that whatever I do there at Island Grill, it was getting me ready for the next step.

Whatever the voice told me to do, I used it as motivation. I always showed up for work on time, I went above and beyond expectations, I helped out my coworkers in whichever way I can, and I finished the job that was assigned to me. In November 2002, the restaurant was having a staff party in Kingston; all the other Island Grill restaurants had combined together for the party. While I was at the party, unexpectedly I heard my name called to the front during the awarding ceremony; I was presented with an award for employee of the year. I was happy with this new job. Instead, I was the lead cook on my shift. I cook food such as jerk chicken, pumpkin rice, hamburger, chicken sandwiches, and chicken soup.

I always enjoyed serving the passengers of cruise ships when they came to Island Grill to eat; they liked the taste and flavor of real authentic Jamaican jerk chicken. But while they sit and eat, the only thing that came to my mind was that one day I'd get the chance to work on one of those cruise ships no matter what happened. Whenever I worked on day shift, after I left work in the afternoon, I always stopped by the Ocho Rios ship pier and watched the cruise ship sail away slowly into the deep ocean. I just imagined myself on a cruise ship one day, standing at the back, looking toward Ciboney, waving my hands to my lovely island of Jamaica.

After I got settled at Island Grill, I went and got a little cheap one-bedroom apartment to rent. Now I had two apartments, one in Clarendon and one in Ocho Rios, where I am staying. But it was very hard to keep up with the two apartments, so I decided to give up the one in Clarendon. At that time, my mother was able to have access to a cellular phone, so I called her and told her to make some space because I was going to give up the apartment in Clarendon, and I would give her the few pieces of furniture that was there. I went to Clarendon the following weekend and took all the stuff to my mother's house. When I got there, Richard wasn't there; he was still at work. But I left him a message even though he was expecting me that day. Also, my mom was very happy to see me.

I went back to Ocho Rios the following Monday; there was this guy at Island Grill by the name of Phillip Graham, who helped to train me at the restaurant while I was on probation. We became friends because of two reasons—first, he helped to train me, and second, he is from Clarendon. He was the only one I came across who came from Clarendon at that time. Also, his mother lived in another community, which was not too far from where my mother lived. We always talked about traveling abroad; as a matter of fact, I've always had the desire to go back to school and get an AA degree or certificate. But one thing I know was that working and going to school was very hard to accomplish in Jamaica; also the school fees are so expensive.

Both of us struggled when we were growing up, even though Phillip got things easier than me because he was living with both his parents. In addition to that, his father usually went to the United States, at least twice per year. Working at Island Grill was good and also rewarding, but as time went by, I realized that I reached a point at my job where I couldn't learn anything new, and that was very frustrating to me. However, that was when I knew that it was almost time for me to take another step up the ladder.

God spoke to me through my inner voice and told me to buy another Sunday Gleaner again and see who was hiring. So I went and did exactly what the voice told me to do; the first section of the Gleaner that I went to was the section that said Career Opportunity, and that was actually in the middle of the Gleaner. While I was there browsing through the career section, I came across a company by the name of Royal Caribbean Cruise Line. The Gleaner says that they are hiring people to work on the cruise ship. The following Monday, I used my cellular phone to call the number; I spoke to a lady, and she told me all the documents I needed to take to the office, along with a fee of fifty US dollars. Then she made an appointment date for me to come to the office and fill out some paperwork.

The same day, Monday, I called Phillip after I was through talking with the lady and told him what the lady told me. Phillip said that he was going to call the office the next day, which was Tuesday. However, he did not call the ship agency, so I went to the ship agency office on my appointment date and completed all the paperwork and paid the fee for processing. After everything was finished, the lady told me that within three weeks, they will give me a call to let me know if my application was accepted or not. But from the first moment I walked into the office, I got this feeling like, this is it, the moment I had been waiting for. As a result of that, my confidence went sky-high; I felt like I just scored a 100 percent on a final exam.

When I first applied for the cruise ship job, it was December 2002; however, it was already by the first week of January 2003 when I got a phone call from the ship agent telling me that my application had been accepted. They set a date for me to come to the office for an interview; on the day of the interview, there were about twelve of us. I had to sit in a room and wait until it was my turn with the interviewer. When it was my time to get interviewed, I was very nervous; my legs and arms were just trembling. Instead, I stood up and took a deep breath in, shook my shoulders a few times, and then walked into the interview room. I walked in that room so strong and confident, you could hear the sound of my shoes from about three office spaces away from the room I was going toward.

The sound of my shoes sounded like this: cum cum cum. Even though I was looking young in my face, I had no choice but to go inside that room and show some authority, show the person who was going to interview me that I was more than capable of doing the job. When I entered the room, there were two gentlemen sitting at a table. I said good morning to them with a vigorous voice. They replied, "Good morning." I stood there for a few seconds. Then one of the men said, "You can have a seat, Mr. Stewart." His name was Randy. I replied to him, "Thank you." I gently pulled my chair out and sat down.

They both tried to interview me at the same time, but I only kept focus on one person at a time. I looked directly in his eyes and answered him "Yes, sir" and "No, sir," depending on what the question was. Then after I finished answering the question from the first person, I then addressed the next person. Although I was nervous at first, the interview went through quickly and smoothly; after the interview finished, they told me that they are going to call me at a later date and let me know if I passed the interview. Within a couple of weeks, my phone rang. I anxiously picked up the phone, and it was the important phone call I was waiting for. I said, "Hello." The person said, "Can I speak to Wilfred Stewart?" I said, "Speaking." The person said, "You have been selected to work on Monarch of the Sea. It will sail out of Miami, Florida, your ticket will cost US $150," I would be staying at the Raddisson Hotel in Miami for one night and then would board the ship the next day. That was the best phone call I ever had back then.

After I got that information over the phone, the next step for me was to go to Kingston for my physical to make sure that my blood and everything else in the body were OK. The agent also made me an appointment to go and get a seaman visa at the US embassy in Kingston. I got my visa and my medical report, and everything was fine. The medical cost me three hundred US dollars. I was looking toward this, so I put some money aside to help pay for the medical because I knew that it was going to cost a lot due to the testing of the blood to check for any disease in the body. So that led to me spending all the money I saved up.

Therefore the only expense I had left was the money for my plane ticket. Even though I spent all my money on the physical, I still have to come up with an idea on how to get the money for the ticket. I was thinking about my daddy because he might have the money, but on the other hand, he might be scared to lend me the money because he might think it was a scam with the ship agency, and he won't get his money back if something like that really went down. Furthermore, I promised that I won't ask my parents for any more money. And then Richard and Mr. Myers, my two good friends, were so far away in Clarendon. I needed the money right now because I had a limited amount of time to get the ticket, and the closest person to me here in Ocho Rios was Phillip. So I went and asked him if he had some money he can lend me to purchase my ticket. He gave me twelve thousand Jamaican dollars, which was two hundred US dollars at that time. I gave him two options on how I would be able to pay him back. The first option was that I would send back the money as soon as I get my first pay check; the second option was I would keep the money until my eight-month contract was completed and I returned to Jamaica.

During that time, Phillip wasn't really worried about me not paying him back; his main concern was it should be the two of us getting ready to leave for the ship. But he didn't want to call and make an appointment with the ship agency; I did not let that stop me. I just kept my eyes on the prize and kept pushing to the end. Everything went through so quickly, I just could not believe it. When I first started applying for this job, it was December 2002. And here I was in February 2003, all set to go and work on a cruise ship. I was so happy and thankful to know that the Lord had blessed me and answered my prayer, and my dream also came true. Even before I left Jamaica, I set the long-term and short-term goals that I wanted to achieve in the future. My short-term goal was to buy a piece of property while my long-term goal was to build a house on the property so that my mother can live there and stop paying rent.

That was the mind-set I really left Jamaica with, and I tried to work toward it very hard. So after having my passport for so long, it was time for it to go to work. I went and booked my flight. So now it was official, when

I was leaving for the ship. My older brother Dixie made arrangements to come to Ocho Rios and pick up my furniture to take them to my mother's house. Then I gave my supervisor at Island Grill two week's notice that I am leaving. They didn't want me to leave because one of the operation managers from the Kingston head office came down to Ocho Rios to have a meeting with me to find out why I was leaving. But nothing could ever stop me from leaving because I already took all my stuff to my mother's house.

Working on the Cruise Ship

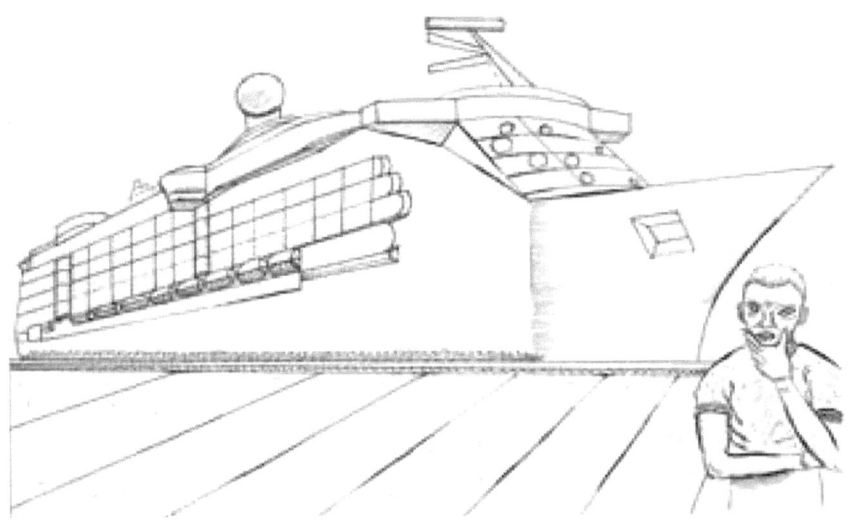

On March 2003, I left Jamaica for Miami, Florida, where I boarded the ship in Fort Lauderdale. My mother accompanied me to the Norman Manley International Airport in Kingston, Jamaica; she was very happy that I got the chance to go and work on a cruise ship. On the other hand, she knew that she was going to miss me, so she started crying and praying for me. Even though I was playing tough, I could not hold it any longer; I just burst out in tears. Nevertheless, we managed to get over the crying, and it was time to check my luggage in and then go through customs. The entire money in Jamaican currency I have left I gave to my mother. The two main reasons why my mom was so worried about me going to work on a cruise ship were because, in the olden days, people said that persons who worked on cruise ship always stayed away from their family for a long period of time before returning. Next, they might get thrown overboard while they are sleeping at night, and finally, the Titanic scenario.

Because of that reason, even my other brothers, sisters, and some of my friends would not take the chance to take a job on a cruise ship; however, I still didn't know if the other stories were true, except for the Titanic. Yet I surely wasn't thinking about those thoughts; moreover I know one thing for sure that once you believe that there is a God, and he sent his only begotten son, Jesus, to come and die on the cross for us because of our sins. I personally put him first, and then I followed his footsteps and moved forward in faith. Traveling on air with Jamaica Airlines was my first time ever traveling on a plane, but I was happy that I got a window seat; that way I could have a good look at the overhead view of the island of Jamaica.

When I was boarding the plane, I could still see my mother waving her hand to me; I waved back to her and went inside the plane. As soon as the plane got off the runway, the first thing that came to my mind was when I was small and heard an airplane pass by, I would always look up and stare at it for a long time until it was far out of sight, and I couldn't see it anymore. As a result of that, I was sitting in an airplane now; on the other hand, some kid might be doing the same thing I was doing when I was small. However, the scene from above was great. I reached Miami, went through immigration OK, and caught the shuttle bus to the hotel where I will be staying for one night. I checked in at the front desk, got my room key, and then went on to find my room number so that I can put down my luggage.

After I found my room and stayed there for a few minutes, I left the room to go and find a restaurant to get something to eat. Staying at this hotel was not the same as those hotels in Jamaica because there weren't a lot of fun activities taking place here compared to the hotels in Ocho Rios, including the last hotel I worked for. Because of that, I didn't stay out of my room for long; I just got some food and went back to my room and watched a movie. Moreover I was tired and sleepy, so I went to bed because the next day, which was a Monday, was going to be a big day for me. I woke up at about 6:00 am on Monday. First, I got dressed, and second, I put all my things back together and then went and ate breakfast. During breakfast time, I met two other guys who were going to work on the same cruise ship as me. One of them was from Montego Bay; the other one was from Clarendon.

After we finished eating breakfast, at 7:00 am, all three of us boarded a bus that would take us to the ship port in Fort Lauderdale. Most of the people that were on the bus were returning crew members while the remaining few were new crew members. As a result, the bus reached the port, and all the new crew members were so excited when we saw that huge ship tied to the dock. Still I couldn't believe that I was so close to a cruise ship that I always watched after I left work in Jamaica. After I got my bag off the bus, I had to wait outside the dock until all the passengers disembarked the vessel. Then someone from the crew office on the ship came and got us outside.

At about 11:00 am, a lady from the crew office came and got me; she took me to the crew office on the ship where I filled out some more paperwork. After I finished the paperwork, then she gave me my room key; next I went and put my bag in the room. Shortly after, it was time for lunch, so I went and ate lunch. Then my new supervisor came and got me; he took me inside the galley and introduced me to the executive chef. He also showed me where my workstation was and explained what my duties were. Then he took me to the main store at the front of the ship where I would be getting my uniforms. My new job title was galley utility (the person who washes all the pots and dishes). From the first minute I put my feet on the ship, the work began; at first I believed I would get the Monday off to get settled in. That wasn't the case; I had to get straight to work. After I received my uniform, I went back to my room where I found out that one of the guys from Jamaica that I met at the hotel was my roommate. Although it was almost time for me to go to work for the first time, I still had to take a little nap. That way I won't feel sleepy at work, and it could enable me to do a good job on the first day. Our beds were bunk beds; however, I was the first one to check into the cabin, so I took the bottom bed.

I was scheduled to go to work at 7:00 pm Monday, but I did not have an alarm clock, so I did not wake on time. At about 7:30 pm, I heard someone knocking on the cabin door; I jumped off the bed and rushed to the door. It was my supervisor who came to get me for work. In spite of me waking up late for work the first day on the ship, there were a few reasons why I could not wake up early. First, I was in a new environment, and second, I did not have a clock to alarm or to look at that time, and finally, everywhere on the ship was pure light, so I could not tell the difference between day and night. I went to work, and there was this guy from St. Vincent who trained me for the first week on the job. By the time I got my first break, the ship was already sailing. Even though the ship was sailing, I could not tell that it was moving until I went to the back of the ship and looked at the water. The ship wasn't rocking at all.

Before my lunch break was over, I met a few more people from Jamaica and other Caribbean islands. So as a result, it felt a little bit more like home. Eating the food on the ship was a big challenge for me; the only thing I could eat were the vegetables and fruits. The majority of the guys from Jamaica worked inside the galley, so most of the time, they cooked some Jamaican or Caribbean food, and they will offer me some to eat. The first week on the ship, I was doing a lot of training and boat drills; the safety officer on the ship took me for a tour of the ship. He showed me all the emergency escape routes, the watertight doors, and the lifeboats and life rafts. He also explained what the emergency signals were and why it was used on a ship and also where the life jackets were located inside the cabins and how to use them in the case of a real emergency situation.

The ship was so huge; it took me two weeks to know all the different areas and locations on the ship: for example, the crew dining room, the laundry room, the theater where most of the trainings and meetings take place, and even my own cabin where I live. The number of guests the Monarch of the Sea carries was about 2,500 passengers and 800 crew members. However, my original workstation was at the deck 4 galley pot wash, even though sometimes I had to go to the windjammer dish wash to help out, sometimes on the first day of the cruise especially the three-day weekend cruise and also the cruise for the Super Bowl finals.

Sometimes when it got real busy and the chefs used a lot of pots and thin sheets, they piled up so high on the table at the pot wash that when someone passed, they can barely see who was working at the pot wash. I remembered one day I was working at my regular station at the deck 4 galley pot wash. The thin sheets that the bakery and the roast cook used to cook on, mainly the cookies, corn bread, and baked chicken, were so dirty sometimes I can't get off the food that stuck on them. Instead I have to put them in a big sink with the water boiling at the highest point, along with a special chemical to help cut the old food off the thin sheets. I took time-out one day to count the entire thin sheets that were at the pot wash, and I counted one hundred thin sheets.

After I finished washing all those thin sheets, I felt like someone strapped two fifty-pound lead on both of my arms. I could barely move my arms the next day. Although I was excited about the ship job, I still would like to get a day off; instead I only get a few hours off whenever the ship comes to port. If I was not working, I would get off the ship in the US port and make a phone call to my family and friends back in Jamaica. The ship only comes to Fort Lauderdale and Key West Mondays and Tuesdays. But sometimes when the ship docks at Fort Lauderdale, I don't get to come off all the time; instead, I was doing some side job or I was scheduled to work at the storeroom to help the storekeeper load the ship with food. I don't get full days off on the ship. The contract that I signed when I first boarded the ship was for eight months, so just imagine working seven days a week for eight months without no real days off and only a few hours to take a nap and make phone calls. On deck one, at the back of the ship where the storeroom is located was like the warehouse and grocery store for the entire ship. It has things such as meat, fish, fruits, vegetable, wine, beer, liquor, ice cream, and dry food. Every Mondays in Fort Lauderdale, the ship was loaded with food. At the storeroom, there was a provision master who controlled the entire storeroom, and then there were another three inventory storekeepers and two utility storekeepers whose responsibility was loading the ship with the food and also the issuing of the food to different locations on the ship, for instance, the galley and the bar.

The Monarch of the Sea was doing a seven-day cruise; it would sail out of Fort Lauderdale. The first stop after it left Fort Lauderdale would be Key West, second was Cozumel in Mexico, third was Grand Cayman, and the final destination was Ocho Rios in Jamaica, and then back to Fort Lauderdale. However, my first time going back to Jamaica on a cruise ship was like a dream come true, something that I was really hoping and praying for. When the ship reached Jamaica with me on it for the very first time, I just could not stop smiling; it was like an adventure for me. And the other passengers and crew members were just as excited as I was because that was the only place when the ship came to port, where everyone tried to get off. Even though the ship was in Jamaica, not everyone from Jamaica will get the chance to get off and see their family and friends. Some of the Jamaicans have to stay and work because they were scheduled.

But some of the supervisors and managers were cool; they allowed everyone to get off the ship in Jamaica, even if they were scheduled to work. That day, I was on time off, so I got off and went to see Phillip at my old job; we talked for a long while about the experience I gained on the ship. Everyone at my old job was very happy to see me again. Most of the people at my old job knew that I no longer work there, but they did not know where I was going to work next. Therefore when they heard that I came to Ocho Rios on a cruise ship, they were astonished. By the time I got back on the ship in Ocho Rios, it was almost time for me to go back to work and for the ship to sail out to sea, so I rushed to my cabin to get dressed for work. After I got dressed, I hurried to the back of the ship where I always saw the other crew members and passengers stand and wave to me when I always came to the pier to watch the ship sail out to sea.

I could not raise my hand; instead, the first place I looked toward was up there in the hills of Ciboney Hotel. And the second thing that came to my mind were those early mornings when I always watched the ship coming in slowly to dock. In addition to that, it was always a good feeling to know that whatever I want in life, I can achieve if I put my heart, mind, and soul into it. And I didn't let anything stop me from getting what I deserved, and I remembered that hard work was the key to success. Anyway, it was time to get back to work in my tall black water boots, dressed in a full suit of khaki and a pair of green plastic gloves stuck tightly in one of my back pockets.

Since I'd been on this cruise ship, I never experienced having seasickness, but I heard other crew members talk about it daily. As the ship headed farther out in the ocean, the water started to get rough and the ship started rocking from side to side, causing everything that sits on wheels to start rolling, a few glass plates by the dish rack got broken. Next, I started to get a headache, then my stomach started bubbling like a volcano, getting ready to erupt. Finally, I rushed to a nearby bathroom; I got there on the right time. I started vomiting some green stuff. It surely doesn't look like anything that I have ever eaten before; that was the worst experience I had on the ship. That was the first and only time it ever happened to me while working on the ship. Getting seasick was not good; the only thing I wanted to do when I got seasick was go to bed and sleep it off. One crew member told me that it usually happened to people who just started working on a ship for the first time, so there was no need to worry if it only happened once.

In spite of what happened, I still won't quit my job because I had my goals that I needed to achieve, yet my plan was to complete it in at least five contracts or less. Working on the ship was fun because on Monarch, there were crew members from at least fifty-two different nationalities. As a result of that, when it came to independency, the crew office gave most of the countries a party at the back of the ship while it was sailing. My job was cool because I got the chance to go and help out the guys at the storeroom on Mondays, which was loading day. But at one point, I had to ask the executive chef for a change because the chemical that I used to wash the pots was cutting my fingers. Because of my experience from Island Grill in Jamaica, the chef gave me another job at the windjammer galley as a breakfast cook. The windjammer galley is located on deck 11.

I worked at windjammer for the remainder of my first contract and then went home for a two months' vacation. Phillip came to pick me up at the airport in Montego Bay; I did not pay back the money I borrowed, but I bought him a pair of Timberland shoes. Then he borrowed $1000 US dollars from me even though I was only making $250 US dollars every two weeks on the ship. Also, I put some money in the bank to purchase a piece of property; however, my entire family was very happy to see me again. I stayed home most of the time I was on vacation, but I also went to see Richard and Mr. Myers. The two months went by very fast; it was time for me to go back on the ship.

I started my second contract, but it was time for the ship to go to the dry dock where the people at the shipyard would take the ship out of the water and work on it; they worked on the entire ship from top to bottom. The ship was so high in the air I could drive a big rig truck underneath it while it is in the air. While the ship was in dry dock, I ended up working in the storeroom; during the time I was working as a galley utility, I always went to the storeroom to help out the storeroom guys. Because of that, the provision master saw the work I did, and he was impressed, so he requested me to work in the storeroom along with the other guys, Sandy, Sean, and Lescut. The dry dock that the ship went to was at a free port in the Bahamas. The ship wasn't going to cruise in the Caribbean region anymore.

Therefore, as the work finished at the dry dock, the company decided to move the ship from Miami, Florida, to California. Because Florida is far away from California, they had to take a shorter route to reach California. But the shortest route they had was the Panama Canal; that was another good experience for me because of the way they pulled the ship through the canal. There was no passenger on board, only crew members; the ship had to arrive at the entrance of the Panama Canal early in the morning and form a line to go through the canal. However, the canal was built like huge series of steps that fills with water. When it was our time to move through the Panama Canal, the persons who worked at the canal attached four strong cables to the ship, two on each side, that also attached to four other equipment that pulled the ship forward.

The Caribbean Sea was lower while the Pacific Ocean was higher; that was how the two oceans appeared because of the way how the canal connected the two. Even though the canal's shape was like a step, it was divided into sections, and each section was higher than the previous one. The entire ship fitted in one section; then the section filled with water. Next, the equipment that was attached to the ship pulled the ship forward. Each time the ship moved to the next section, the ship got higher, and the water ran out from the previous section and filled the next section. However, the process kept on going until the ship reached the level of the Pacific Ocean and was ready to sail by itself.

The Panama Canal was a shortcut that many shipping companies used to get from the Caribbean Sea to the Pacific Ocean or vice versa. Therefore the Panama Canal saved companies a lot of money and time. If Monarch was to go around the Caribbean Sea to the Pacific Ocean, it would take us about two weeks and some days to reach California. During the trip through the Panama Canal, I came close to a couple of countries such as Costa Rica and Nicaragua. The ship reached California safely even though the water was very rough; my cabin was on deck 0, and sometimes when the wave hit the ship, it sounded like someone was using a stone hammer and ponging the ship. Although my second contract finished so fast, I could not believe it, but I was able to do a little shopping this time. I bought a few things for my family this time around. I went to see Richard and Mr. Myers again; Richard still worked at the grocery store while Mr. Myers was still teaching at Ebony Park. Phillip always picked me up from the airport. And we both were talking about investing some money into pig rearing. At first it sounded like a good idea; the day before I went back to the ship, I gave him money, US $250, and he went and bought a boar and a mature female sow. He bred the sow, and she produced an offspring of twelve piglets. He was rearing the pigs by his mother's house because they had a big property. By the time the pigs reached maturity and were weighing fifty pounds, I was back in Jamaica on vacation again. I asked Phillip to get one of the pigs slaughtered so that my family could get some meat to eat.

The day when the pig was slaughtered, I gave half of the meat to Phillip's family and took the other half with me home and gave some to my neighbors. However, in the year 2005, I went back to the ship for another contract. But in the month of February 2005, it was Super Bowl weekend, where a lot of people came to the cruise ship to watch the Super Bowl finals. During my second contract on the ship, I was able to get some side jobs; that was the reason why I could afford to do some shopping for my family and friends. Moreover, I was comfortable and relaxed, and I also knew my way around the ship. However, one of the side jobs was to take the passengers' bags from their room door to deck 1 at the end of each cruise. Because the Super Bowl cruise was like a party cruise, the safety officer on the ship always increased the presence of security at the disco at night.

As a result, I got the job to work as a security at the disco during the night. Sunday night was when we took all the bags down to deck 1 and got them ready to get off the ship on Monday morning. The port that we used was in San Pedro now that we were in California. While I was taking the bags from the passenger area, there was this lady coming toward me; she came up to me and asked me what the latest time the bags had to be outside the cabin door was. I told her twelve midnight; then we continued talking for a while. As a result of our talk, I ended up asking for her phone number, but she left and went back to her cabin. However, it was time for

61

me to go and take up my security duty at the disco. There was this other guy from Jamaica that was helping me collect the bags, and I told him, "I am leaving because I have to go and work at the disco, but if a lady came by looking for me, tell her that I asked you to collect the number from her." And I left for the disco.

After I left, she came back and gave my friend the number; my friend came to the disco and gave me the number. As soon as the disco finished, I went straight to my cabin and called her. We talked for a long time, and that was when I knew what her name was Alice M. Wilson. I could not get off the phone with her even though I was tired and needed to get some rest because I had work in the morning; nevertheless, we got off the phone and went to bed. In the morning, she got off the ship and went home. Since that night, we both kept in touch with each other. Every Monday and Friday when the ship goes to San Pedro, San Diego, and Catalina Island, I'd call her, but I mostly called her in San Pedro. It was closer to her home and also more convenient for me. Sometimes she came to pick me up in San Pedro, and we went out to have lunch.

One Monday, she came and got me at the ship pier in San Pedro; we went to have breakfast. After we finished eating, she took me to meet some of her family members such as Redman, Pam, Ella, Jack, and her mother. Then it was time for me to board the ship again; while she was taking me back to the ship, she asked me what my plans were. I told her that my plan was to buy a piece of property in Jamaica and build my mother a house on it so that she could stop paying rent. On the other hand, before I started working on the cruise ship, I did not have a serious relationship with any female because when I was ready to settle down, most of the ladies that I met were young, and they weren't ready to have a serious relationship yet. And moreover, I was working on the cruise ship; I only went to Jamaica for two months out of a year, so it was hard for me to have a relationship going while I was away on the ship. Based on the question she was asking me, I knew where she was heading. However, she was also single, so we were both on the same page relationship-wise. As a result of that, we decided to give it a try and see where it'd take us. Everything was going fine; she would make sure she would come and get me whenever the ship came to San Pedro every Monday when I got my time off. The ship came to San Pedro on Fridays, but that was the day when we loaded the ship with food, so I could not come off the ship to see her on Fridays. I told her that I didn't want to get into any trouble here in the States or even in my own country, so I told her that if she really wanted to get me into the United States, she would have to call US immigration and ask them what kind of paperwork she needed to file for in order for me to get to the United States. She got in contact with immigration, and they told her about the fiancé visa, so she went and filed for it. While the papers were being processed, my contract was up, so it was time to go back to Jamaica for another two months' vacation. During my vacation, my older brother Dixie introduced me to a man who had some property that he was selling.

The man was an elderly person who was also getting very sickly. The amount of land he had that he wanted to sell was two acres. However, I bought the property for eight thousand US dollars. Although the money that I got working on the ship wasn't a lot, I had to make some sacrifices to save that amount of money. It also took discipline and dedication to know what I want and stick to it. After I purchased the Shop property, I still had a little extra money left, so one day while I was on my way to Frank field, I saw a sign on a building that said for Rent. I took out my cellular phone and called one of my sisters from my mother's side and asked her if she would sell some snack in a shop.

She said yes. I then went and contacted the owner of the property, who was a man. He said that it was OK for me to rent the shop; I paid for the first two months' deposit on the shop. On the other hand, the shop needed a little repair, so I helped my sister Clover to put some more shelves and a counter in the shop. The first day the shop opened, it made some good sale even though it was a Sunday. But it was close to a doctor's office and the Edwin Allen High School in Frank field. During that time, my girlfriend, Alice, was expecting my son, Alex, in 2005. I returned to the ship to start my fourth contract within the third week of January 2006. I received a phone call from Alice. She told me that she got a letter in the mail, saying that the fiancé visa was ready and waiting at the US Embassy in Jamaica for me to collect.

As a result, I went to human resources on the ship and told them that I had an emergency in Jamaica, so I asked for some time off to go home. Usually the company bought my ticket whenever the contract was finished and it was time to go home, but now because it was an emergency, I had to come up with the entire money for the ticket. I came up with half the money, and the company put the next half. I left for Jamaica on February 13, 2006. When I reached Montego Bay Airport, Phillip was already there waiting to pick me up. We talked on our way to his house; he did not mention anything about the pig that we were rearing. On the other hand, I did not ask him anything about it either. I left his house in Montego Bay early the next morning and went to the US Embassy in Kingston because of the long journey from Montego Bay to Kingston. When I got there, the section that I needed to go to was all ready closed.

I had no idea that my trip was going to be like this; I took another transport and headed to my mother's house. On my way there, I saw my stepmother at a shop, sitting down; I asked the vehicle that I was in to slow down a little, and she asked me why I came back so quickly. I told her the reason; then she told me that there was a letter for me at the post office where she worked. At that time, she was on her break. I asked her to take it home with her, and I would come and collect it when she got off work in the evening. Then I went to my mom's house. When I got the letter, it was from the US Embassy. The letter was telling me all the steps I needed to take in order to get the fiancé visa. That way I could start gathering all the important documents I needed, and I didn't have to go back to Kingston until I had them all. No one was expecting me except Phillip and my mother because I'd just left Jamaica in December 2005, and now here I was again in February 2006, and I normally stayed on the ship for eight months. While I was going back and forth trying to get all those papers, I found out that Phillip had sold all the pigs, and my sister Clover closed down the shop because it wasn't making enough money for her to do her personal stuff. There were a few reasons why I tried to open the shop. First, I might not always be in the position to send money for my mother to buy food, so by having a shop, she can get some food or grocery from it. And second, another family member can get a job working in the shop, and the third and final reason was I didn't want to be at the same level at all times. So I was hoping that the shop would make enough money to get a bigger building and then extend it to a minisupermarket.

As for Phillip, he was the one who lent me the money when I was going on the cruise ship for the first time, so I thought this would be a good way to show appreciation to someone who helped me out when I was in great need. But the only good thing was that I did get some meat from one of the pigs. On the other hand, I was there struggling to find some money to do all these paperwork. Even though I struggled a little bit, I managed to complete all the paperwork and took them to the embassy on my appointment date and was able to get the fiancé visa. I also had to do another physical and blood test to make sure that I was in good shape. After everything was final at the embassy, I had to wait five days before the fiancé package was delivered to me by a courier service.

Everything went through OK, and I got my fiancé visa; I then left Jamaica for the States in April 2006, but this time, not on the cruise ship. From the day I entered the States and was accepted by US immigration, I had ninety days to get married and file the rest of the paperwork. We got married in June. After the papers were sent off, I had to stay at home and wait for my work permit to come in the mail. However, staying at home was very hard for me because I never stayed at home for such a long time; I was always out working or looking for work. But sometimes I would get out of the house and take a walk around a couple of blocks so that I can get myself acquainted with the surroundings in which I live.

Within a month or two, I got back a reply from immigration for me to go for a biometric fingerprint and some other interviews. During that time, I was at home; I was watching a lot of television. One day, I was just flipping through the channels to find a sports channel. While I was flipping, I came across this channel that was doing a commercial for the Art Instruction School in Minneapolis, Minnesota. My inner voice told me to pick up the phone and give the school a call; I followed the voice as usual and called the school. They took all the necessary information from me; in a week's time, I received a letter from the school in the mail. In the letter, they sent two images for me to draw and send back to the school; I looked at the image very carefully and drew it next to the original image. After I finished with the drawing, I mailed it to the school. Next, they sent me another letter; this time, it was the score from the drawing I did. I scored 90 percent on the drawing.

In November 2006, I received my permanent residency card. I did not hesitate; I went out and started looking for jobs, but it was hard to get a good job at first; therefore I just wanted to do something and be a man. The first job I got was at a fish market; the name of the fish market was

Alex Fish Market, on Martin Luther King Jr. Boulevard, Los Angeles, California. I was working there in the daytime, but after I completed the first three months there, I got another job with this company named Neutragena. The first job at the fish market started at 8:00 am while the second job started at 11:00 pm, so I was able to work the two jobs while catching the bus to work. One Sunday in December 2006, I was at home when I heard the doorbell ring, I went to see who was at the door, and it was a man from the art instruction school in Minneapolis. He told me that he was a representative for the school, and he came to talk to me about the program so that I can get a full understanding of it. I invited him inside the house, and he outlined the course to me and my wife.

She was happy for me; she told me to go ahead and take the course if I liked it. However, the man told me that this course was a distance education course. Instead of sitting in a classroom, I would study at home on my leisure time. He also told me that there were a lot of people who took this first drawing test, but he can only take time out to come and visit the people who got a very good grade, and I was one of those whose grade was high. So that's why he was there to talk to me; moreover, when he looked at the drawings, he could see that I had good control of the pencil. And I had the potential to become a better artist in the future. In spite of what he told me and the outcome of the two images that I drew, I took the course; it took me about eighteen months to complete it. As a result, I got my certificate in drawing fundamental.

Catching the bus was not easy because everywhere I wanted to go, I had to leave the house at least one hour in advance in order to get there on time. So I decided to go to the DMV, and I took a test to get my driving permit so that I can take a few driving lessons. One weekend in 2007, my wife and I were at the gas station, pumping some gas in her car. While I was pumping the gas, there was this guy on the other side walking to his car, but he was facing us. He was wearing a light-blue shirt with short sleeves and a button at the front; the shirt also had a Pepsi logo at the front. My wife turned to me and said, "That's a good company to work for." Immediately I went over to the person and asked him if Pepsi was hiring; he told me that he didn't know, but the best thing I could do was go to the Pepsi website and fill out one of the application and see what happened from there, and moreover the summer holiday was coming up, so I stand a good chance of getting in.

After we reached home, my wife went on the computer and went to the Pepsi website and filled out the application. One week later, she received an e-mail from Pepsi saying that they received my application, and they were in the process of looking over it. Within a week or two, she received another e-mail; this one was saying, "We are sorry, but after we looked over your application, it didn't meet the criteria that we were looking for." Although this wasn't the answer I was looking for, now was not the time for giving up hopes because I had been through some rough times in the past that prepared me for times like these. However, my inner voice talked to me again. But this time, I wanted to talk it out, and I needed somebody as my witness, so I told my wife that whatever they were going to do or say, I really didn't care, but the only thing that I knew was that this job belonged to me, and I was going to get this job no matter what it took or how long it took. By May 2007, my wife got another e-mail from the Pepsi Bottling Group telling us that they looked over my application a second time, and they saw that I had experience in the warehouse and was asking if I was still available for this position.

I responded to the e-mail, and I was scheduled for an interview with Victor Coronado; the interview went through OK. However, the next step for me was to go for a physical and then the orientation. I passed everything and got the job; then I started working at the Pepsi production plant in Torrance, California. I started the job on June 7, 2007. I also gave up the other two jobs because the job at Pepsi was more demanding, but the benefit was very good for my family. And it was a good-paying job, so I had to make a decision on which job to keep, and I made the right choice.

In 2009, I decided that I wanted to continue with my art study, so my wife introduced me to this community college with the name El Camino. I went to the administration office to get some information about how to get enrolled in the school. I got all the information that I needed. After that, I went to the school's website and filled out the application form and submitted it. Next, I received my student ID number, and then I went and did the placement test. As a result of that, I started attending El Camino in summer of 2009; the first class I took was drawing fundamental. I had to take this class as a prerequisite for the other art classes; this time, I got the chance to sit in the classroom with other children and the professor as opposed to the art instruction school where I had to stay at home and study.

In the meanwhile, I was going to school and working full-time at Pepsi; it was a little easier because I got my driver's license and was able to buy myself a little car from one of my wife's cousin for seven hundred US dollars. So now I didn't have to catch the bus anymore. It wasn't anything fancy, but the bottom line was it took me where I wanted to go—mainly school and work. The car was a 1989 Toyota Camry; I called it colorless because the color on the outside had burnt out. The next class I took at El Camino College was in fall of 2009. I knew that I wanted to take my art skill further, but I still wasn't sure what art field or area I wanted to launch out in. But for now, I wanted to take a chance with studio art; I went and took this digital art class. On the first day of class, I was late because I had just left work and went straight to class; the professor asked me why I was late. I told her the reason why even though she was just getting ready to go over the course syllabus with the class so that it was clear to everyone.

After she was through with the syllabus, next she roll-called to see who showed up for the class and who needed to be added to the class. Every student whose name was called must go and sit next to a computer; then she finished calling the names and every student who registered for the class had a computer, and if there were any left, the rest of students could register based on how much computer was left because the class required each person to have their own computer. When everything was settled, I told the professor that I didn't have a lot of experience working with computer; she asked me what I could do on the computer. I told her that I can turn on the computer and maybe type a few words. She told me not to worry; she would help me.

As the class progressed, she got another student who was more computer literate to come and assist her with students who had less computer knowledge. The person that she got was a guy by the name of Robert Guerrero. Robert would always make sure that I wasn't falling behind in the class. The class was good, but I wasn't really looking for a big grade because this was my first time using a computer in a classroom, so I took it as a learning process and a starting point. Yet I pushed myself to the limit, and I still finished the class with a C grade at the end of the semester.

After the semester had finished, I was able to buy a laptop computer and downloaded a couple of thirty-day free trial from the Adobe website. So when I was at home in the summer, I can get some practice and get more comfortable with the computer. I did not take any more summer classes because the classes met four days a week, and during the summer, at my job, that's when it got busy. However, the free trial that I got had Photoshop and Illustrator. By the time it was spring, I was far more comfortable than the first time when I took the digital art class. So now I signed up for two classes instead of one; the two classes that I was taking were digital photography and publishing/design. This time, I had a different professor; her name is Joyce Dallal. She taught both classes that I was taking.

The photography class was cool; I took a lot of pictures with the camera from different angles and positions. I also learned how to use the low shutter and the high shutter speed on the camera, how to make a panorama and surreal picture. While in the publish/ design class, I learned how to design posters, business cards, book layouts, and cover designs. We also worked on the 2010 Myriad book for El Camino College.

While I was taking those two classes, I thought I was more comfortable in the photography class than the design class. So I was looking to get at least a B in the photography class and maybe a C in the other class. But unfortunately, things did not work the way I thought. Instead it was the other way around; I got a C in photography and a B in publish/design. As a result of that, I said to myself, How could this be possible? I really felt like I mastered the photography class more.

The Lord talked to me loud and clear this time and told me, "Look, you take this publish/design class, and you help to design a couple of books, so now is your time to write a book about the things you went through in life to reach this point in your life today." So it was after I took those two classes that I got inspired, and I started writing this book in 2010. On the other hand, I only worked on the cruise ship for three years and was still work with Pepsi even though right now, January 17, 2012, as I was typing this line of text, I was laid off from my job at Pepsi. What can I do but give God thanks for health and strength. Also, I was building a little house for my mother in Jamaica.

A MESSAGE

I, Wilfred Stewart, would like to take this time-out to send this message to all the kids out there attending school. We all know that going to school is a little stressful at times, but I am here right now to tell you that education is the key to success. It is a very important piece of tool to have; if you don't use that piece of tool today, you surely are going to use it tomorrow or sometime in the future. But first, you have to know and believe that there is a God that loves us all, and next you have to respect and obey your parents. The Bible says that you must honor your mother and father, and your days will be longer on this earth.

The same respect goes for your teachers in the classroom and the elders on the street, at home, on the bus, or wherever they may be because they are the ones who set the foundation for me and you. And please don't go to school because your parents send you to school or because you want to show off your new shoes or a new phone. Go because you want to achieve something good in life for you and your family and also to let your parents feel proud about you. One of my favorite Jamaican singer song goes like this, "Book book book, you must pressure your book." And that was really cool of him saying that in his song. Because reading is knowledge, and knowledge is power. I believe in building more schools and paying teachers more money; also if there are any kids out there who like to tag property or write graffiti, that means you have the potential to become an artist. And you should be taking some art courses at a school. When I look and see what some kids had to go through in school in other third world countries, for instance, Jamaica, some schools don't even have their first computer as yet. And the kids here have everything at the tip of their fingers. The only thing I am asking you to do is to use the opportunity that you have now to the fullest extent. To anyone who reads this book, please reach out to the next person closest to you and tell him/her to take school seriously or go back to school.

Also to the parents, they have this little quote that says, "The best teaching or the best school begins at home." We all love our kids, but we need to have a boundary between love and discipline because they will abuse the love that you have for them. Sometimes a little whipping is good, even the Bible tells us that "we must not save the rod of correction, and spoil the child." Sometimes we need to make random check at the school and even on their backpack before they leave home in the morning or when they get home from school in the evening. Check for homework/assignment; let the kids spend more time reading books and less time playing games, only if it is educational.

It is not nice when the police is the first one to whip a child; sometimes it is caused by something that the child brings, says, or does at home. It may be very simple, but because we, the parents, don't stop it, it leads to the police whipping our child and putting them in jail. The next thing I want to point out to all the students is going to school. Why take a weapon to school? The only heavy-duty weapon a child should carry in their backpack to school is a Bible, and it should contain several live scriptures that shoot through the devil, from Genesis to Revelation. That is all you need to fight the biggest battle.

I don't write this book for fame or success; I write this book for the children to become successful. And last but not least, I could not have written this book without mentioning this great legend by the name of Bob Marley because when the time got rough and tough, I always sing his song that goes like this, "Don't worry, about a thing, for every little thing, is gonna be all right."

www.ingramcontent.com/pod-product-compliance
Lightning Source LLC
LaVergne TN
LVHW041545070526
838199LV00046B/1835